Blazing the Economic Freedom Trail

Edited by Robert Carling

Connor Court Publishing

Blazing the Economic Freedom Trail
Edited by Robert Carling

Published in 2026 by Connor Court Publishing Pty Ltd

Connor Court Publishing Pty Ltd
PO Box 7257
Redland Bay QLD 4165
sales@connorcourt.com
www.connorcourt.com

The Centre for Independent Studies
Level 1
131 Macquarie St
Sydney
NSW 2000

Printed in Australia

ISBN: 9781923568266

Front Cover Design: Karla Pincott

50 years OF IMPACT

THE CENTRE FOR INDEPENDENT STUDIES

Contents

Prologue: What Goes Around Comes Around

Robert Carling

Economic ideas were key to the founding of The Centre for Independent Studies in 1976. The context both globally and in Australia was stagflation and increasing government intervention in economic affairs. Australia had just experienced the economic vandalism of the Whitlam government.

More fundamental than an economic cycle or the coming and going of one government, however, the classical liberal recipe for economic stability and progress had failed to catch on in the battle of ideas over the long period of post-war Keynesian consensus — but in the 1970s was about to strike back.

In the mid-1970s a classical liberal revival was taking shape thanks to the intellectual leadership of people like Milton Friedman and Friedrich Hayek. The CIS sought to apply their economic ideas to the Australian context. A global trend became established following the elections of Margaret Thatcher in 1979 and Ronald Reagan in 1980.

In Australia, the advocacy of the CIS and allies bore fruit from the mid-1980s and there followed a long period during which policies of governments from both sides of the political divide gave practical expression to beliefs in market principles, free trade, competition, low inflation and fiscal discipline with tax and government spending restraint. Although far from complete, the conversion was substantial and long-lasting.

Well into the first decade of the new century it seemed that the battle of economic ideas had been won by free market and smaller government adherents. But as a sharp reminder that no battle of ideas is ever won forever, it is becoming increasingly evident that in important respects we are now back to where we were in the 1970s. Many of the subsequent economic reforms remain, but others are either under challenge, in retreat or gone at least for the time being. What goes around comes around.

Just when the set-back for classical liberal economics started and what caused it are not sharply defined. Some say it was the Global Financial Crisis of 2008-09. Whenever or whatever, this has become the contemporary context of CIS's work on economic affairs — and it is reflected in the reports and op-eds that make up this chapter which mostly date from around the time of the GFC

The seven sections start, appropriately, with the fundamentals of economic freedom — including a defence of the capitalist (or market-based) economic system and papers rejecting some of the major attacks on that system since the GFC including modern monetary theory and the idea of a universal basic income. This leads to a section on regulation, red-tape and how to get Australia out of its productivity slump.

The next sections cover government spending and in particular social spending that has been the main driver of bigger government. This leads naturally to a section on taxation, which as the main way government exercises its coercive power over citizens has been a key area of interest by CIS.

The last two sections cover housing and superannuation, which are perennials of the Australian economic policy debate.

Fifty contributions from more than 20 authors stretching back more than 20 years, condensed to their essence, make for an impressive compendium. Sadly, a few of the authors have passed away and many are no longer part of CIS other than as members and friends who still follow our work. But this collection stands as a sample of a much larger body of work on economic issues under the CIS umbrella over an even longer period. Apologies to other authors whose important contributions have not been included. Where we have included works from the distant past, it is because the issues they discuss remain salient today.

While there is a high degree of consistency across the contributions, there are differences of view. CIS does not attempt to promulgate a corporate view and is happy to publish different points of view based on sound scholarship that advances freedom and individual liberty.

What is consistent, however, is the advocacy of economic freedom and the rejection of economic planning and other manifestations of unwarranted state intervention in free markets. While the issues may vary, the battle of economic ideas is as intense now as at any other time since the founding of the CIS.

Section One: Foundations of Economic Freedom

Robert Carling

This chapter brings together a series of essays that confront some of the most persistent misconceptions shaping contemporary debates about economic policy. At a time when confidence in market economies is wavering, and when ideas once confined to the margins—such as degrowth, Modern Monetary Theory, and universal basic incomes — have moved into mainstream discussion, clear-headed analysis is essential. These pieces offer exactly that: accessible, rigorous examinations of the principles that underpin economic prosperity, the errors that recur in arguments against capitalism, and the consequences of policies that promise much but deliver little.

Across these contributions runs a common thread: the reminder that prosperity is neither accidental nor inevitable. Market economies, grounded in voluntary exchange, entrepreneurship, and the rule of law, have been central to the remarkable improvements in global living standards over the past two centuries. Yet those achievements risk being taken for granted. As several of the authors note, misunderstandings about how wealth is created, and how public spending is ultimately financed, can lead to policies that undermine the very foundations of growth.

The chapter also highlights the intellectual drift in public debate — from evidence-based analysis towards proposals driven by wishful thinking or political expediency. Whether in calls to abandon growth, claims that governments can spend without limit, or arguments that inflation stems from corporate greed, there has developed a disregard for the institutional and behavioural realities that shape economic outcomes. By contrast, the works reproduced here insist on a return to first principles: sound incentives, prudent fiscal management, openness to innovation, and an appreciation of the limits of state intervention.

Together, they form a timely reminder that prosperity requires more than good intentions. It demands economic literacy, institutional discipline, and the courage to challenge fashionable but flawed narratives. Readers will find in the following pages both a defence of the market economy and a practical account of the policy choices Australia must make if it is to secure sustainable growth in the decades ahead.

Why we should defend capitalism Summarised

Robert Carling

Introduction

The market economy, or capitalism, is the foundation of prosperity for developed nations like Australia, supplying essential goods and services, jobs, and income. The core principle, derived from Adam Smith, is that individuals acting in their own self-interest generate mutual benefit. Despite its proven record, capitalism has become controversial, with critics including world leaders and a concerning 58% of Australian millennials holding a favourable view of socialism. Capitalism is defined as an economic system where the means of production is privately owned to generate profits, and its resilience comes from its compatibility with the democratic rule of law.

The system's greatest achievement is the dramatic reduction of global poverty. The proportion of the world's population living on less than $2 USD per day has fallen from 94% two centuries ago to less than 10% today. This rapid decline in extreme poverty saw millions of the global poor join the middle class, and was accompanied by vast improvements in health and nutrition. For example, life expectancy in the UK rose from 30–40 years to over 50 by 1900.

Economic development and capitalism are also strongly associated with women gaining legal rights and equality. Economic autonomy, facilitated by the market economy, is a key precursor to equal rights. In Australia, women now represent over 50% of lawyers and over 40% of medical practitioners, demonstrating that their participation in the market economy has been vital to these advancements. The United Nations' Human Development Index further shows a strong correlation between gender equality and higher-income countries.

The observed rapid population growth over the past two centuries is not an issue but rather a symptom of increased prosperity, primarily because improved nutrition and advances in modern medicine have allowed more people to survive to adulthood.

Capitalism in Australia

Australia's sustained prosperity is largely attributed to market-oriented reforms implemented by successive governments from the 1980s to the early 2000s. Key reforms included the privatisation of government assets — such as the Commonwealth Bank, Qantas, and Telstra — and the establishment of the National Competition Policy. These actions fostered competition and drove productivity growth, leading to the system that provides consumer choice from private companies.

Common criticisms of capitalism

Despite the clear benefits, capitalism is frequently and incorrectly targeted as the cause of various problems in Australia. However, failures like excessive greed and unethical behaviour, such as those exposed by the Royal Commission into financial services, are often mistakenly blamed on capitalism. Fundamentally, the welfare system and its social expenditure programmes are entirely reliant on the revenue collected from businesses and workers employed in the market economy. Therefore, capitalism is the essential bedrock of prosperity that enables the social welfare system to exist.

Conclusions

The market economy has become the dominant global system, yet it is facing diminishing favour among younger generations in Western countries, with 58% of Australian millennials holding a favourable view of socialism. While market economies can be successfully combined with generous social benefits, as exemplified by the Nordic countries, this is only sustainable because the necessary revenue is generated by the market economy itself. Capitalism is the indispensable foundation of prosperity and is essential for maintaining the social welfare system.

This has been adapted from a 2018 Centre for Independent Studies research paper. The full paper can be found at https://www.cis.org.au/publication/why-we-should-defend-capitalism/

I, Mechanical Pencil:
Why a socialist economy can never work

Steven Kates (2019)

Introduction

The paper revisits Leonard Read's classic 1958 essay *I, Pencil* to explain why socialist economies fail. Read's original story showed how the manufacture of something as simple as a pencil depends on the coordinated efforts of thousands of people worldwide, none of whom intend specifically to make pencils. This spontaneous coordination arises from market processes, not government control. The paper updates the story through the perspective of 'I, Mechanical Pencil', arguing that the loss of economic freedom under socialism inevitably brings both political oppression and poverty. Read seeks to show why prosperity depends on the mechanisms of a free market and how socialism destroys them.

The Story *I, Pencil* Told

Read's pencil described itself as the result of innumerable individual decisions — from miners in Sri Lanka to shipbuilders and factory workers — all linked through voluntary exchange. The miracle was that no single mastermind directed these actions, yet the 'invisible hand' of the market coordinated them to produce a pencil. Kates agrees with this lesson but expands on how the process works in practice. The production of even the simplest goods requires dispersed knowledge, incentives, and coordination that only market prices and private enterprise can provide.

Understanding How Things Work

Modern societies enjoy prosperity without understanding how it is created. People see goods and services flow towards them but mistake this for a natural condition rather than the product of countless entrepreneurial decisions and voluntary exchanges. Without this understanding, they risk undermining the very processes that make prosperity possible. Every improvement, from wooden pencils to modern mechanical ones, reflects human innovation operating through market systems, not miracles or government design.

Making the Invisible Hand Visible

Six elements are essential for a functioning market economy:

1. **Entrepreneurs** – individuals who take initiative, deciding what to produce and bearing personal risk.
2. **Finance** – enabling entrepreneurs to pay for inputs before earning revenue.
3. **The Price Mechanism** – freely set prices that guide resource use efficiently.
4. **Profits** – rewarding success and signalling what consumers value.
5. **Government** – providing sound rules rather than directing production.
6. **Property Rights** – protecting ownership from theft and political interference.

Remove any one of these, Kates argues, and prosperity collapses.

The Errors of Socialist Theory

Socialism reverses each of these principles. It substitutes central planning for markets, allocates finance politically, imposes price controls, suppresses profit motives, and undermines property rights. Each measure alone would cause economic stagnation; combined, they guarantee disaster. Historical experience, he argues, confirms that centrally directed economies always end in scarcity and repression.

The Entrepreneurs, Finance, and the Price Mechanism

Entrepreneurs and financiers drive productive activity through risk-taking and discipline imposed by potential loss. Without the freedom to fail, efficiency and innovation vanish. Market prices transmit crucial information about scarcity and cost, guiding producers to minimise waste. When governments fix or distort prices, shortages and inefficiency inevitably follow, as seen repeatedly in socialist systems.

Profits, Government and Property Rights

Profit ensures that the total value of goods produced exceeds the resources used — the essence of economic growth. Governments, by contrast, do not create wealth but establish the legal and institutional framework allowing markets to function. The protection of private property underpins both personal freedom and capital accumulation; once the state confiscates wealth through taxation or nationalisation, investment collapses, and living standards fall for all.

The Process of Change

Innovation is constant, and market economies adapt continuously as entrepreneurs commercialise new ideas. Prices and profits provide the signals that drive this evolution. A socialist system, with its rigid planning and political control, suppresses such dynamism. Only an open market allows the continual adjustment that sustains rising prosperity.

Signing Off

Understanding the economic processes symbolised by a pencil is crucial to preserving freedom. The market economy — built on entrepreneurship, profit, and voluntary exchange — is the true source of both liberty and material progress. Any attempt to replace it with socialism, however idealistic, will destroy both.

This is an edited extract of a 2019 Centre for Independent Studies research paper. The full paper can be found at https://www.cis.org.au/publication/i-mechanical-pencil-why-a-socialist-economy-can-never-work/

Debunking Degrowth

Gene Tunny (2023)

Introduction

The degrowth movement calls not just for abandoning economic growth but for shrinking economies to reduce humanity's environmental impact. Advocates include environmental activists such as Extinction Rebellion and some ecological economists who blame growth for climate change, pollution, species extinction, and resource exhaustion. Degrowth would mean an intentional contraction of economic activity and acceptance of significantly lower living standards, enforced through heavy restrictions on personal freedoms and markets.

Although once a fringe idea, degrowth is gaining academic and media attention. Prominent figures such as Jason Hickel, Tim Jackson, and Kohei Saito have popularised it, while some academics have modelled it as a climate-change strategy. However, implementing degrowth would be socially and economically devastating, undermining liberal democracy and prosperity. The paper reviews the principal claims made by degrowth proponents and shows they are largely unproven.

The Degrowth Movement

Degrowth asserts that economic growth is causing irreversible damage to the planet and risks human civilisation. It is defined as "a planned reduction of excess energy and resource use to bring the economy back into balance with the living world". Supporters argue that growth cannot be decoupled from environmental harm and that continued consumption will lead to collapse.

The movement draws on earlier ideas such as Kenneth Boulding's 1966 "Spaceship Earth" concept and the later "steady-state" and circular-economy schools. However, degrowth goes further by rejecting any reconciliation between current living standards and environmental limits. Tunny identifies five key, but unproven, claims made by the movement and addresses each in turn.

Unproven Claim 1: We Need to Degrow to Stop Climate Change

The Intergovernmental Panel on Climate Change does not advocate degrowth, and modelling of mitigation policies shows economies still growing — though perhaps at slightly slower rates. Australian Treasury analysis suggests that pursuing net-zero emissions would still leave national income over twice as large by 2050 as today.

Degrowth advocates rely on worst-case scenarios from climate models, but leading scientists such as Judith Curry, Steven Koonin and Bjorn Lomborg highlight the deep uncertainty around such projections. Moreover, rapid advances in clean technology — artificial intelligence, renewable energy, electric vehicles and battery storage — indicate that innovation, not contraction, is the more plausible route to decarbonisation.

Unproven Claim 2: We Need to Degrow to Stop Resource Depletion, Environmental Degradation and Biodiversity Loss

Degrowth activists argue that even a transition to net zero cannot prevent ecological disaster. Tunny counters that environmental conditions are improving in many areas thanks to conservation policies and wealth. The Living Planet Index shows that about half of monitored wildlife populations are increasing. Wealthier, democratic nations typically achieve better environmental outcomes, a pattern consistent with the Environmental Kuznets Curve.

The premise that growth inevitably worsens pollution is mistaken: societies can change production methods and use market-based instruments — such as carbon taxes or emissions-trading schemes — to internalise environmental costs. Historical successes like the Montreal Protocol's phase-out of ozone-depleting chemicals illustrate this.

Concerns about resource depletion are also unfounded. Higher prices encourage conservation and exploration, as shown by Julian Simon's famous wager with Paul Ehrlich. Fears of "peak oil" likewise proved false: global output has continued to rise.

Unproven Claim 3: We're Rich Enough Already

Proponents such as Hickel claim rich countries should stop growing because additional wealth adds little to wellbeing. Tunny replies that growth remains vital for developing economies and for eradicating poverty. Since the late 1970s, market-oriented reforms in China and India have lifted more than a billion people out of extreme poverty. Economic growth also correlates strongly with higher life expectancy.

Economists, far from worshipping growth for its own sake, recognise trade-offs and environmental limits. As the Australian Treasury noted in 1973, policy should aim at efficient resource use and community preferences rather than arbitrary GDP targets. Degrowth's caricature of economists as believing in infinite growth 'regardless of the costs' is therefore inaccurate.

Unproven Claim 4: We Need to Degrow to Reduce Inequality

Degrowth advocates link capitalism and growth with rising inequality, but Tunny observes that global inequality has actually declined as emerging economies have grown. Between 1975 and 2010, the global Gini coefficient fell markedly as more than a billion people escaped poverty.

While inequality has widened within some rich countries, wealthier societies possess more capacity to redistribute income and address social issues. The freedom and opportunity generated by market economies remain essential to human flourishing, as emphasised by Friedrich Hayek. Reducing growth would diminish that capacity without guaranteeing equality.

Unproven Claim 5: We Need to Degrow to Avoid Economic and Social Collapse

Modern warnings of impending collapse echo the 1970s *Limits to Growth* thesis, which assumed fixed resources and ignored innovation. Later studies claiming its accuracy merely confirm past trends, not the forecasted collapse. Economic projections by Nobel laureate William Nordhaus suggest per-capita GDP will keep rising over the century, with only a minimal probability of global decline. There is therefore no empirical justification for enforced economic contraction.

Implications of Degrowth

Achieving degrowth would require unprecedented state control over private life—restrictions on work, consumption, travel and production. In growing populations, this would mean higher unemployment, welfare dependency and social unrest. No democratic government has adopted such a policy because it would be deeply unpopular and authoritarian.

Degrowth would also reverse the remarkable gains in global living standards and poverty reduction achieved since the 1980s. As Robert Solow noted, the only path to a decent life for developing regions is more total output, not less. Market-based environmental policies and protection of property rights offer more effective, liberal solutions.

Conclusions

There is no sound reason to pursue degrowth as a policy goal. It relies on dubious assumptions, ignores the role of markets and innovation, and misrepresents economics. While humanity must manage environmental risks responsibly, prosperity and sustainability are not mutually exclusive. Degrowth would impoverish societies, restrict liberty, and undermine progress. The movement is simply the latest form of pessimistic doom-mongering. Humanity has repeatedly overcome resource and environmental constraints through ingenuity; this time will be no different.

This is an edited extract of a 2023 Centre for Independent Studies research paper. The full paper can be found at https://www.cis.org.au/publication/debunking-degrowth/

Degrowth proponents wrong to claim capitalism causes climate change

Simon Cowan and Gene Tunny (2023)

Despite continued optimism from the government, and the lowest unemployment level in half a century, economic times are tough in Australia. Cost of living pressures have soared, and the aggressive action taken by the Reserve Bank to curb inflation has smashed mortgage holders and economic growth.

Our extended period of positive economic conditions no doubt made many complacent, but the turbulent past 18 months has underscored the importance of good economic management. Our quality of life is strongly connected to controlled and sustainable levels of inflation, rising productivity and strong economic growth.

The declining economy has also underscored the folly of those calling for a radical abandonment of the pursuit of economic growth in order to combat climate change. These calls come from environmentalists, including activists in groups such as Extinction Rebellion, and some economists, particularly in the field of ecological economics.

Degrowth proponents say economic growth is to blame for climate change, pollution, species extinction, and resource exhaustion. They think the only solution is a contraction of economic activity and an acceptance of permanently lower living standards. In short, they believe we must abandon capitalism and actively shrink our economy because continued growth is not, as one 'degrowther' put it, "compatible with the physical reality of the planet".

The degrowth movement is gaining attention worldwide, has international conferences dedicated to it, and tenured academics are supporting or contemplating it. However, degrowth is based on several assumptions and conjectures that are highly suspect and lack evidence, particularly regarding a speculative ecological collapse or various catastrophes associated with climate change. These assumptions inform computer simulations which to a significant extent assume the Doomsday they are forecasting.

Nor does degrowth consider the positive role markets play in ensuring efficient resource use. As resources become scarcer, the price increases, encouraging conservation or exploration for new resources or alternatives. Market-based mechanisms, possibly including carbon taxes, can play a role in correcting external costs imposed on the environment by industry. Well-defined and enforced property rights are also important. For instance, rainforest conservation efforts in Brazil have been hampered by "lawlessness", as reported by The Economist earlier this year.

In addition, as the bulk of economic activity worldwide occurs in the private sector, achieving degrowth would require the implementation of a range of highly restrictive policy measures that would constrain private decision-making. In effect, it would require central direction of how much people could work and consume. It may require restrictions on travel, such as bans on driving on allocated days if your number plate has particular digits, as been done in Beijing. Climate lockdowns and 15-minute cities may be conspiracy theories for now, but it is very unlikely degrowth could be achieved without radical authoritarian policy measures — far more than was seen during the pandemic.

Even in wealthy countries like Australia, a policy of degrowth would cause widespread poverty from declining employment and consumption; with its related costs in social welfare and social ills such as crime and homelessness, among others.

There are real climate issues that need to be addressed, but degrowth is not the answer for several reasons. First, credible modelling of climate change mitigation shows economies still growing as we transition to net zero, although substantial investments need to be made in decarbonisation. In other words, there is no need for as drastic a step as degrowth to meet the challenges identified.

In fact, the degrowth movement seemingly deliberately ignores the substantial progress that has been made to arrest environmental degradation worldwide, suggesting that theirs is an ideological position rather than a practical one. It is perhaps not that surprising that the idea has gained traction among those who have always been hostile to capitalism.

Second, economic growth is strongly connected to innovation, and it is to innovation that we must look to solve complex problems like climate change. Degrowth by contrast is a throwback to the ideas of Malthus and the kind pessimistic doom-mongering that humanity has seen many times before. Productivity and innovation have repeatedly pushed us beyond what were previously considered hard constraints of growth.

Third, the degrowth movement would deny those living in poverty around the world the improvements in living standards that come with economic development. One of the great achievements of the past 30 years has been the lifting of over a billion people out of poverty worldwide, particularly as China and India moved away from the anti-market economy and the Licence Raj respectively. Between 1990 and 2019, the proportion of the world's population living in the most extreme poverty, on no more than US$2 per day, has fallen from around 38% to 8%, according to World Bank data.

It is important to understand that, while degrowth itself remains something of a fringe position, the thinking underpinning it is far more widespread. The idea that capitalism is the cause of climate change, and that we need to fundamentally remake the economy to combat it, has a lot of traction among young progressives in particular. But this position is a good example of what Rob Henderson calls luxury beliefs: "ideas and opinions that confer status on the rich at very little cost, while taking a toll on the lower class".

In fact, you could go further and suggest that many holding this view simply do not understand how devastating this policy would be in practice. Our current economic hardship would pale in comparison. Abandoning capitalism, growth and innovation in the name of ecological purity would condemn us all to poverty.

This opinion piece was originally published in 2023 by *The Canberra Times.*

The MMT Hoax

Tony Makin and Gene Tunny (2021)

Introduction

Modern Monetary Theory (MMT) has entered public debate as an alternative macroeconomic framework claiming that governments issuing their own currency need not worry about deficits or debt, since they can always create money to fund spending. Its popularity owes more to political appeal than academic acceptance. Economists from both conservative and progressive schools, including Paul Krugman and Larry Summers, have rejected its central tenets.

MMT gained prominence through Stephanie Kelton's *The Deficit Myth* (2020), which argues that taxes and spending should be managed to balance the overall economy rather than the budget. She claims money is simply created electronically when central banks make payments on behalf of the Treasury. The theory has resonated during periods of economic distress such as the Global Financial Crisis (GFC) and the COVID-19 Crisis (CVC), when fiscal stimulus replaced monetary policy as the dominant stabilisation tool. MMT contends this approach should be permanent.

The paper evaluates MMT's economic validity and warns that its adoption would produce worse outcomes than the problems it seeks to solve.

Everything Old Is New (and Wrong) Again?

MMT is essentially a re-packaged version of 1930s Keynesianism, not a new paradigm. Its ideas echo early Keynesian and Post-Keynesian theories advanced by Joan Robinson, Paul Davidson and Abba Lerner, blending "old, corked Keynesian wine in a newly labelled bottle." Keynes's original model ignored the role of money and central banks, later integrated by John Hicks through the IS-LM framework.

During the post-war decades, fiscal policy dominated economic management, based on the Phillips Curve's supposed trade-off between unemployment and inflation. However, this belief collapsed with 1970s stagflation, prompting the Monetarist and New Classical revolutions led by Milton Friedman, Robert Lucas and Thomas Sargent. Their work exposed the limits of discretionary fiscal policy and the importance of monetary discipline.

Subsequent theories by Mundell and Fleming showed that for open economies with mobile capital and floating exchange rates, fiscal stimulus raises exchange rates and trade deficits rather than domestic output. Supply-side economists such as Arthur Laffer further demonstrated how high taxes and welfare discourage work and enterprise. MMT, by ignoring these developments, reverts to pre-1970s ideas.

MMT rests on four main propositions:

1. Capitalist economies naturally operate below full employment.
2. Deficit-financed public spending should boost demand to close this gap.
3. Budget deficits and debt are harmless because governments can always create money.
4. Inflation, if it occurs, should be controlled by raising taxes, with fiscal policy dominating monetary policy.

Each proposition is critically assessed in the following sections.

Chronic Unemployment?

MMT assumes chronic under-employment caused by insufficient demand, reviving Alvin Hansen's "secular stagnation" hypothesis. Yet after World War II, advanced economies achieved strong growth and low unemployment through trade and productivity gains. Even after the GFC, the United States reached near-full employment before the pandemic due to pro-growth, supply side policies

Low investment, not inadequate consumption, explains weak growth in many countries. In Australia, sluggish private investment has limited productivity and wage growth. MMT's definition of full employment — near-zero unemployment — ignores the natural rate arising from frictional and structural factors. Economists such as Friedman and Phelps showed that pushing unemployment below this level with demand stimulus only fuels inflation. For Australia, the natural rate is about 5%, achievable only through labour-market reform, not deficit spending.

Extra Government Spending?

MMT's prescription of permanent fiscal expansion implies an ever-growing public sector. Like Keynes, MMT disregards distinctions between productive and wasteful spending, and assumes economies are closed to trade and capital flows. In open economies such as Australia's, deficit spending increases imports and widens the trade deficit rather than boosting output.

Moreover, unconstrained public spending risks inefficiency and 'white-elephant' projects. Evidence also shows that excessive government size hampers long-term growth by crowding out private investment and creating uncertainty about taxes and debt.

Monetising Budget Deficits Not a Problem?

MMT advocates direct monetary financing of deficits, asserting that governments can print money without consequence. History disproves this: from Rome to Weimar Germany, excessive money creation led to hyperinflation. While modern central banks have employed quantitative easing (QE), this differs from MMT because monetary authorities retain independence and can later unwind asset purchases.

MMT would subjugate central banks to government control, eroding the independence that was vital to conquering inflation in the 1980s and 1990s. Linking large fiscal deficits with rapid monetary expansion would ultimately unleash inflationary expectations difficult to reverse.

Public Debt Not a Problem?

Contrary to MMT claims, mounting public debt raises interest rates, undermines confidence, and may trigger bond-market instability, as in

1994. Global debt reached about 225% of world GDP before COVID-19 and rose sharply afterwards. Japan's debt — 250% of GDP — illustrates the stagnation that follows excessive borrowing.

Australia's general government debt is projected to double from 42% of GDP in 2019 to about 80% by 2024, threatening its AAA credit rating. Much of this debt is held by foreign investors, causing income outflows that reduce national income and competitiveness. Monetising deficits under the pretext of "monetary sovereignty" would jeopardise Australia's low-inflation credibility.

Could Higher Taxes Curb Inflation?

MMT proposes using taxation, not monetary policy, to control inflation. This assumes governments can fine-tune demand swiftly and precisely — an assumption discredited since the 1970s. Legislative delays, inequitable effects, and distortions to incentives make tax adjustments an impractical inflation-control tool.

Higher taxes would depress work effort and investment, shrinking supply and productivity. With half of Australians paying little or no net tax, effective anti-inflationary tax rises would fall on lower-income households, worsening inequity.

A Drag on Productivity

By promoting the state as 'employer of last resort', MMT risks reviving unproductive public employment that plagued Australia before the 1980s. Such policies demand higher taxes and reduce efficiency. They also invite politically motivated 'nation-building' projects — such as the Snowy Mountains Scheme, the Ghan railway, or school-hall programs — without rigorous cost-benefit analysis. Ignoring fiscal constraints encourages waste and drags on long-term productivity.

Conclusion

MMT commands little academic credibility. By disregarding history and empirical evidence, it repeats errors that produced past inflationary crises. Countries practising MMT-like policies—Argentina, Venezuela and Zimbabwe—illustrate the consequences: chronic deficits, hyperinflation, and economic decline.

Australia's adoption of MMT would mean larger government, heavier debt, higher taxes and weaker growth. MMT is not a 'Modern Monetary Theory' but a 'Mistaken Macroeconomic Theory'— a 'magic money tree' illusion promising prosperity through printing presses but leading instead to inflation, inefficiency and lost economic freedom.

> This is an edited extract of a 2021 Centre for Independent Studies research paper. The full paper can be found at https://www.cis.org.au/publication/the-mmt-hoax/

UBI – Universal Basic Income is an Unbelievably Bad Idea

Simon Cowan (2017)

Executive Summary

The concept of a Universal Basic Income (UBI), defined as a government payment to its citizens with minimal restrictions, has existed for a long time but has gained significant momentum in recent years. Supporters on both the political right and left, particularly those in the technology industry, advocate for its adoption. However, the central argument for a UBI — that it is necessary to address widespread technological unemployment — is fundamentally flawed and does not justify such a far-reaching government intervention.

Technological change has historically created more labour opportunities than it has destroyed. Furthermore, modelling of a UBI demonstrates that it would be extremely difficult, if not impossible, to implement effectively without causing substantial harm. A UBI model that provides a payment to everyone and leaves current welfare recipients no worse off would require hundreds of billions of dollars of additional taxation. Alternatively, a UBI funded by reassigning existing welfare payments would inevitably undermine the payment's universality or result in vulnerable citizens receiving significantly less income.

Technological unemployment and the movement towards a Universal Basic Income

Technological unemployment is a theory asserting that automation and technological change will lead to a permanent reduction in the overall demand for labour. This justification for a UBI has become increasingly popular as the effects of globalisation and automation have moved beyond blue-collar industries to potentially threaten white-collar workers.

The history of technological change and labour markets suggests that such change does not justify sweeping government intervention like a UBI. Historically, technological progress, such as the period of the Luddites in the 18th century, has been marked by innovation leading to a massive creation of new types of jobs, thus refuting the notion of permanent technological unemployment. The underlying logic is that if productivity increases, then real incomes rise, resulting in greater demand for goods and services, which in turn creates new jobs to meet this demand.

The primary concern is not that people will be unable to find work, but that they may not want to re-enter the labour market following redundancy. However, studies of redundant workers from the 1990s and early 2000s show that most return to employment, with only a minority becoming long-term unemployed. Furthermore, while underemployment and part-time work have risen, data from the Australian Bureau of Statistics indicates that the proportion of part-time workers who prefer to be full-time has not increased substantially. This suggests that workers are not being forced out of full-time work but are adapting to the changing labour market.

Predictions that up to 40% of current jobs are at risk from automation often fail to account for the fact that only a fraction of any given job is suitable for automation, and they do not adequately analyse the new jobs that will be created by technological change.

UBI on trial: does it reduce incentives?

The limited evidence from trials does not provide a robust answer to whether a UBI would reduce the work incentive. The incentive problem is a major concern, as the UBI would remove the existing requirement for many welfare recipients to actively seek work.

Canada

The Mincome experiment in Dauphin, Manitoba, in the 1970s is often cited, but the limited study results show that only two groups significantly reduced their working hours: new mothers and teenage boys, who stayed in education longer.

Finland

The Finnish UBI trial was not a true UBI, as it was only provided to a limited group of unemployed people. As the trial excluded those in work, it was fundamentally unable to test whether a UBI would reduce the incentive to work.

Modelling a UBI: Type 1-A payment to all

A Type 1 UBI would pay a basic, universal amount to all citizens, from children to pensioners, with a basic rate of $15,000 per year to adults and $7,000 per year to children. This model requires the abolition of nearly all existing income support payments, with a few exceptions like the Disability Support Pension and the Carer Payment.

To ensure no existing welfare recipient is worse off, the cost of this UBI would be $405 billion. Since only $172 billion is saved from the abolished welfare payments, an additional $233 billion is required to fund the UBI.

Problems

The total additional taxation required to fund the Type 1 UBI is $233 billion. This equates to approximately 20% of GDP, requiring a significant increase in the tax burden.

Such an increase in taxation would be economically disastrous. To raise this sum through the personal income tax system, the basic marginal tax rate would need to be raised to approximately 50%.

If the basic UBI rate is reduced to $10,000 per year for adults, the additional tax required would still be $137 billion. Such a low payment would require the reintroduction of numerous supplements to prevent the most vulnerable from experiencing a drastic reduction in their income.

A UBI restricted to the working age population would violate the principle of universality and would create an arbitrary distinction between those receiving the UBI and pensioners.

Modelling a UBI: Type 2-reassigning existing welfare

A Type 2 UBI attempts to be budget-neutral by reassigning the funding from most existing welfare payments to a UBI payment. This limits the annual payment to $10,000 per adult and $5,000 per child.

In this model, 56% of existing welfare recipients would be financially worse off, and the majority of the benefits would flow to non-recipients. The largest losers would be those on the Age Pension, Newstart Allowance, and Disability Support Pension.

Problems

The inherent flaw of this budget-neutral model is that it substantially reduces the income of the vulnerable citizens it is intended to help. The flaws in this UBI model clearly outweigh the flaws in the existing welfare system.

Winners and losers

The primary beneficiaries would be low-income workers whose UBI payment is greater than their current welfare payments. However, any increase in their overall income would be primarily offset by the increased taxation required to fund the UBI.

In the Type 2 model, the majority of welfare recipients would be worse off, while many people not in the workforce and not currently receiving a payment would benefit.

Recipients of the Parenting Payment would be significantly worse off under both UBI models, which is unacceptable for a payment designed to support the caring of children.

Many young people who are ineligible for Youth Allowance due to parental income or a short duration of time in the workforce would receive a benefit under a UBI, thus providing a payment to a group not currently defined as in need.

The core conclusion is that a UBI is too expensive to implement if it is to leave current welfare recipients no worse off. Consequently, any affordable UBI would have a devastating impact on those who need support the most.

Conclusion

The implementation of a UBI would be nearly impossible because it either requires hundreds of billions of dollars of additional taxation or undermines the universality of the payment while causing current welfare recipients to be worse off. Even if the money could be found, the economic distortions caused by the massive tax increase would create significant difficulties.

The idea of a Universal Basic Income (UBI), a government payment to its citizens with minimal restrictions, has gained popularity but rests on a flawed justification of technological unemployment. The modelling demonstrates that implementing a UBI would be extremely difficult, either requiring a massive, economically damaging increase in taxation or substantially undercutting the income of the most vulnerable members of society. Therefore, a UBI is deemed an unbelievably bad idea.

This is an edited extract of a 2017 Centre for Independent Studies research paper. The full paper can be found at https://www.cis.org.au/publication/ubi-universal-basic-income-is-an-unbelievably-bad-idea/

Voting for a living: A shift in Australian politics from selling policies to buying votes?

Robert Carling and Terrence O'Brien (2018)

Introduction

This paper explores the hypothesis that growth of government has become self-sustaining through the emergence of a segment of the population that both enjoys sufficient direct support from government and is large enough that political parties shape policies to curry its favour.

The researchers used the Australian Bureau of Statistics' latest fiscal incidence study to identify numbers of 'net benefit recipients' as a proportion of those of voting age. Net benefit recipients are (roughly speaking) those who receive greater government transfer payments in cash or kind than they pay in income tax and indirect taxes. ABS data on public sector employment were added to the numbers of net benefit recipients, and the results suggest Australia now has a significant majority of the voting age population comprising net benefit recipients and government employees.

The paper suggests hypotheses derived from the 'voting for a living' theory that predict how policy making in Australia is changing. Observations consistent with all these hypotheses seem common in recent times. Notwithstanding many of these hypotheses, taken individually, undoubtedly have other contributory causes. But 'voting for a living' predicts them all and lends credibility to the fear that Australian democracy has entered a dangerous period of failed policy processes and consequent serious policy mistakes.

The 'voting for a living' theory

The core premise of the 'voting for a living' theory is straightforward: if an individual or household receives a net transfer from the government — meaning the total value of public benefits and services they receive exceeds the total taxes they pay — they have a strong incentive to vote for the political party that promises to maintain or increase that net transfer. Over time, as the proportion of the population reliant on government for a positive net fiscal benefit grows, political parties may strategically focus their platforms on appealing to this large, economically motivated block. This results in a democratic process that prioritises the distribution of wealth and favours higher levels of government spending and taxation.

What would we see if Australia is now 'voting for a living'? 10 hypotheses.

1. Political parties will emphasise policies relying on public expenditure growth, and favour income redistribution over economic growth.

2. Proposed policies from all parties will increasingly favour tax increases targeted on a diminishing minority who pay tax in net terms on their income from private employment; especially tax increases on the disenfranchised and unpopular, such as 'rich foreign multinationals', or 'big banks'.

3. As political parties seek to sustain expenditure growth on a majority—with tax increases on only a diminishing minority—they will become more short-sighted, understating the risks of demographic ageing, protracted fiscal deficits, a build-up in national debt and of a future international slowdown. Voters will be led to believe, if only by misdirection, that their net benefit receipts are secure in any event.

4. As political parties compete for the support of the median voter, the tendency will be for government taxes and transfers to grow to favour the middle of the income distribution—even those with significant private income.

5. Policy development by political parties will become increasingly a matter of exaggerating benefits to the median voter, disguising costs to net taxpayers, and supressing analysis that shows policy will not meet

its stated purpose. Consequently, public inquiry, competent social cost-benefit analysis, and contestable advice will all tend to decline.

6. The gap between the politically-stated purpose of policies and the actual outcomes of those polices may progressively widen. For example, policies purporting to support the disadvantaged may primarily fund service providers rather than correct the source of the disadvantage.

7. Major parties will tend to 'double down' on past policies, either without analysing past outcomes or despite evidence they have demonstrably failed.

8. Voting blocs of public employees will become more influential in party politics. Teachers will support not only more spending on education, but also more on nurses, police, ambulance staff and fire services. The state-owned broadcaster will support them all. This natural mutual support within the public sector will gain institutional strength from all these areas of employment being heavily unionised.

9. As public employee and public sector union influence becomes more politically influential through 'voting for a living', consequences may emerge not only in growth in public employment numbers, but also in relatively fast public sector wage growth and in generous, pace-setting terms of public sector employment.

10. State and territory governments will experience the forces noted in #1 to #9 above no less than the Commonwealth, and those jurisdictions with the largest public sectors may develop the foregoing policy trends faster than jurisdictions with larger shares of private employment and greater proportions of net taxpayers.

Any of these hypotheses, taken individually, may have some other contributing cause or causes as well as 'voting for a living' and the political responses to it. But the 'voting for a living' theory is striking in its potential to explain all 10 observations, and also the changing 'tone' of Australian political debate, with more fractious 'zero sum' debate about distribution and less of constructive 'positive sum' debate about raising incomes for all.

Measuring the forces 'voting for a living'

To test this theory empirically, the methodology for measuring the population that receives more than they pay requires assessing both sides of the fiscal ledger for different households: the total taxes paid and the total value of government benefits and services received.

Net benefits

The determination of "net benefits" is central to the analysis. Data from a fiscal incidence study is used to calculate a comprehensive measure. This calculation includes not only direct cash transfers (like welfare payments or pensions) but also the imputed value of non-cash government services received, such as healthcare, education, and social housing. This total benefit figure is then compared against the total burden of taxes paid by the household, including direct income tax and indirect taxes like the Goods and Services Tax (GST) and excise duties. A household is defined as a net beneficiary if its total imputed benefits exceed its total tax payments.

Changes over time

The analysis is made dynamic by tracking the proportion of net beneficiaries over several decades. The core of the problem is the expansion of the welfare state and the increasing scope of government services, which has steadily increased the number of people who, by design, receive a net fiscal transfer. A growing proportion of the electorate becoming net beneficiaries over time strengthens the political power of this group and intensifies the incentive for politicians to 'buy' their votes.

Public employment

Public sector employment represents a specific and important element of the net benefits calculation. Public employees receive direct wages from the government, and the authors note that these wages are funded entirely by tax revenue. While these individuals pay income tax, the fact that their entire income stream originates from the state makes them a group whose direct economic interest is tied to the maintenance and expansion of government spending and employment levels. The size of this public sector workforce is therefore another measure of the forces potentially driving the "voting for a living" dynamic.

Bringing it all together — the 'voting for a living' population

The measurements of net beneficiaries and the public employment workforce are combined to arrive at a comprehensive estimate of the total 'voting for a living' population. These two groups overlap (e.g., a public servant who also receives a family tax benefit), but collectively, they represent a very large segment of the electorate whose immediate economic well-being is positively linked to the scale of government activity. This combined population is deemed to be large enough to wield decisive electoral power.

Evidence of voting for a living

The paper reviews political behaviour and budgetary outcomes for evidence supporting the theory. This includes assessing the rise of political pork-barrelling, the abandonment of genuine tax reform, and the consistent growth of overall government spending relative to the size of the economy (GDP), regardless of which political party is in power. The evidence suggests a structural difficulty in reining in spending or reducing taxes, a political paralysis consistent with the need to placate a large net-beneficiary electorate.

What is to be done?

While recognising the political difficulty of reversing this trend, the paper proposes solutions that aim to reduce the incentive for 'voting for a living' without dramatically cutting essential services. The ultimate goal is to re-establish a majority of net taxpayers — people who pay more in tax than they receive in benefits — thereby shifting the political incentive back towards policies that prioritise efficiency, lower taxes, and broader national economic growth. Potential solutions might include:

- Transparent enumeration of the problem and debate about it, of the kind this paper aims to carry forward.
- Sharpened inter-generational fiscal modelling to show how an irreversible downward spiral of bad policies increases the risk of economic crisis.
- Renewed focus on broadening tax bases, flattening progressive rates and lowering or eliminating the income tax-free threshold.
- Renewed focus on removing middle class welfare in the forms of transfers in kind which contribute disproportionately to the middle deciles of the income distribution being net beneficiaries rather than net taxpayers.
- Tighter means testing of benefits.
- Lowering the share of government spending in GDP.
- Shifting the political competition away from spending more on education, health and the like to a focus on the effectiveness of current levels of spending.
- Putting a lid on public sector employment and the strong growth in its pay and conditions.

A little of the above is being done, but it is more the case that Australia is now set on the path of increased taxation — if not explicit, then by stealth through personal income tax bracket creep. If there is to be any reduction in the 'voting for a living' population in the years ahead, it will be a result of increased taxation across the board. However, it is hardly the best way for it to come about and is likely to be temporary as growth of spending on government benefits reasserts itself as the dominant force in the longer term.

This is an edited extract of a 2018 Centre for Independent Studies research paper. The full paper can be found at https://www.cis.org.au/publication/voting-for-a-living-a-shift-in-australian-politics-from-selling-policies-to-buying-votes/

Fiscal Reform to Rescue our Future: The 'national conversation' on budgets, spending and tax

Robert Carling (2023)

Introduction

There has been a critical shift in the Australian government's narrative on its finances. Following the May 2022 federal election, the incoming government changed the official line from projections of a gradual path toward a balanced budget and declining debt to one emphasising persistent deficits and burdensome debt. While this shift was partly a political strategy to blame the previous government, it was mostly driven by more realistic economic assumptions. The government failed to take decisive corrective action but foreshadowed a 'national conversation' about economic and fiscal challenges and choices. This necessitates a deeper analysis of Australia's spending and taxation structures to facilitate genuine fiscal reform. Among the issues that should be canvassed in the public discussion of these issues are:

- The level and nature of risks presented by the public debt burden and how these need to be managed over the years ahead.
- The implications of the desired path of public debt for the budget balance — whether projected deficits are sustainable and how rapidly they should be reduced.
- Projections of aggregate government expenditure and revenue and comparisons with past norms.
- The relative contributions of expenditure and revenue trends to projected budget deficits.
- The main sources (by program) of growth in government expenditure.

- The optimal assignment of expenditure and revenue responsibilities between the federal and state governments.
- Identification of expenditure programs that are failing to meet their objectives, and the scope for reforms to make them more effective.
- To the extent that expenditure growth is the cause of fiscal pressures, the scope for reducing it while making expenditure more effective.
- To the extent that revenue is inadequate, identification of the best ways to raise more.
- For a given level of revenue, how the tax system can be reformed to make it more consistent with criteria such as efficiency and equity.

The fiscal problem

Australia faces a structural fiscal problem characterised by persistently high debt, ongoing budget deficits, and a reliance on narrow revenue sources. This problem worsened significantly due to substantial spending in response to the COVID-19 pandemic. The nation needs to move beyond simply talking about balancing the books and instead look at the fundamental determinants of the structural fiscal problem that we have.

Expenditure trends and composition

Despite being smaller than the OECD average, Australian government expenditure has exhibited a clear upward trend over recent decades.

- **Growth Drivers:** The main driver of this persistent expenditure growth is social benefits, which have expanded as the population ages and as governments have introduced new transfer and support schemes.
- **Historical Context:** A level of around 25 per cent of GDP is a reasonably consistent benchmark in the history of federal spending, although it has been lower at times. Now, the budget is heading for a figure 2 to 3 percentage points above that unless policy action is taken to prevent it.
- **Future Outlook:** Key areas like the National Disability Insurance Scheme (NDIS), aged care, and defence spending are projected to place upward pressure on future budgets, threatening to lock in a new, higher baseline for government spending.

Revenue trends and composition

Analysing the sources of government revenue shows that Australia's tax mix is heavily reliant on direct income taxes, particularly personal income tax and company tax.

- **Historical context:** On a long-term view, federal tax receipts have never exceeded 24.2 per cent of GDP and are now approaching that peak again.
- **Reliance on Income Tax:** Heavy reliance on personal income tax has long been seen as a key flaw in the tax system. After some very limited relief from that, bracket creep is projected to take us back to a state of over-reliance on personal income tax.

The aggregates in per capita terms

When government expenditure is analysed on a per capita basis, rather than as a percentage of GDP, the trends become even clearer and more concerning.

- **Real Growth:** In real, inflation-adjusted terms, government spending per person has grown substantially over the last few decades, exceeding the rate of economic growth. This demonstrates that the growth in the size of the Australian state is structural and not merely a reflection of a growing economy.
- **The Problem of Spending Creep:** Even small, seemingly innocuous yearly increases in per capita spending aggregate rapidly over decades, compounding the fiscal challenge and making it significantly harder to achieve balanced budgets without major policy intervention.

Conclusion

Government expenditure is growing faster than the economy and revenue is running at historically high levels. The paper calls for an immediate and honest national conversation about fiscal reform, stressing that fixing the budget requires:

1. **Structural Expenditure Control:** Subject existing and new spending

to close scrutiny with the aim of removing low priority programs and reforming others to strengthen effectiveness and efficiency with a clear focus on results rather than inputs.

2. **Tax Reform:** To focus not on raising more revenue but on restructuring the tax system to achieve better alignment with criteria of economic efficiency, incentive, fairness, simplicity and sustainability.

In these ways expenditure excesses can be squeezed out of the budget over time. The tax burden eased, and deficits brought down.

This is an edited extract of a 2023 Centre for Independent Studies research paper. The full paper can be found at https://www.cis.org.au/publication/the-national-conversation-on-budgets-spending-and-tax/

Strengthening Australia's fiscal institutions

Stephen Kirchner (2013)

The deterioration in the federal government's fiscal position reflects a failure to adhere to a rules-based framework for fiscal policy to guide spending and tax decisions. Fiscal policy has been distracted by the pursuit of macroeconomic stabilisation objectives that are inconsistent with the institutional design of Australia's overall macroeconomic policy framework. An independent central bank pursuing an inflation target, combined with a floating exchange rate, renders the change in the budget balance as a share of GDP from one year to the next an irrelevance from a cyclical perspective.

The government's spending and tax decisions still have important microeconomic and efficiency implications that in turn influence long-run economic growth outcomes. A failure to balance the budget over time can be costly in terms of the burden of public debt interest and the need to increase future taxes in the absence of offsetting expenditure restraint. The cost of public sector borrowing is not just the interest rate on outstanding government debt, but the efficiency cost of future tax increases needed to repay the debt. Expectations for the future path for net debt can undermine confidence even if current levels of debt are low by international standards.

There is a growing international trend towards the adoption of independent fiscal institutions coupled with legislated fiscal policy rules. Local and international experience shows that independent fiscal institutions and fiscal rules, both individually and in combination, can lead to improvements in budget outcomes.

The Australian experience

The deterioration in the federal government's fiscal position reflects a failure to adhere to a rules-based framework for fiscal policy to guide spending and tax decisions.

Fiscal policy has been distracted by the pursuit of macroeconomic stabilisation objectives that are inconsistent with the institutional design of Australia's overall macroeconomic policy framework.

An independent central bank pursuing an inflation target, combined with a floating exchange rate, renders the change in the budget balance as a share of GDP from one year to the next an irrelevance from a cyclical perspective.

Why do we need fiscal rules?

- The government's spending and tax decisions still have important microeconomic and efficiency implications that, in turn, influence long-run economic growth outcomes.
- A failure to balance the budget over time can be costly in terms of the burden of public debt interest and the need to increase future taxes in the absence of offsetting expenditure restraint.
- The cost of public sector borrowing is not just the interest rate on outstanding government debt, but also the efficiency cost of future tax increases needed to repay the debt.
- Expectations for the future path for net debt can undermine confidence even if current levels of debt are low by international standards.

International experience

There is a growing international trend of adopting independent fiscal institutions coupled with legislated fiscal policy rules.

Local and international experience show that independent fiscal institutions and fiscal rules, both individually and in combination, can lead to improvements in budget outcomes.

Australia should draw on this local and international experience to strengthen its fiscal institutions to better address both the current structural budget deficit and long-term fiscal challenges arising from an ageing population.

What should be done to improve fiscal rules?

- An independent statutory Fiscal Commission should assume responsibility for formulating the fiscal and economic parameters that frame the government's tax and expenditure decisions.
- The commission should also monitor and enforce a new set of legislated fiscal rules.
- These rules include limits on the budget balance, net debt, revenue and expenditure as a share of GDP, along with a rule limiting real growth in federal expenditure on an annual basis.
- The remuneration of all Members of federal Parliament should be reduced by 1% for every percentage point breach of the fiscal rules for the duration of the breach.
- A rules-based fiscal policy regime also provides a framework through which policymakers can focus on reducing the size of all levels of government in Australia to 30% of GDP and below to be achieved over 10 years, as proposed by the CIS.

This is an edited extract of a 2013 Centre for Independent Studies research paper. The full paper can be found at https://www.cis.org.au/publication/strengthening-australias-fiscal-institutions/

'Greedflation' myth hides real causes of inflation

Simon Cowan (2023)

With much fanfare, the ACTU has initiated an "Inquiry into price gouging and unfair pricing practices" to be chaired by Professor Allan Fels. Claiming that "corporate profits have been a major driver of inflation", it "aims to recommend practical and effective measures to curb price gouging and protect the financial interests of all Australians".

The ACTU is not the first to try to sheet home blame for inflation to the corporate sector. However this view, dubbed 'Greedflation', fundamentally mistakes cause for effect, leading to a distorted understanding of inflation and ineffective or retributive policy solutions aimed at policing corporate behaviour.

There are big holes in the Greedflation hypothesis. The biggest is that Greedflation has no causal mechanism. As a general rule, companies always act to maximise their profits. Their prices are set in accordance with that goal. Therefore profit margins don't just suddenly rise across whole industries and countries at the same time for no reason. If corporate greed is the cause of inflation, something must have fundamentally shifted the bargaining power of companies vis-a-vis consumers.

Some have pointed to corporate opportunism from supply-side blockages as a result of the pandemic and energy price increases from the Ukraine war (what you might think of as supply side inflation). But these factors would increase production costs and therefore *decrease* profit margins in the short term, not increase them. Many businesses are not able to pass on all the increased costs to consumers, much less larger increases in prices. So, did companies just suddenly all agree to become greedier in late 2021? Have they become slowly less greedy across 2023 as inflation has come down?

On the contrary, there is a good explanation for why corporate profits have risen, that also explains why inflation is high and unemployment is at historic lows. Excessive fiscal and monetary stimulus across the world in 2021 (especially the second half of 2021) caused an excess of demand in the economy. That shift in demand resulted in some extra production (more jobs). However, as the rise in demand exceeded the productive capacity of the economy, companies could charge more for their goods. The profit maximising behaviour of companies meant higher prices (inflation) and higher profits.

'Greedflation' is not the cause of the current mess, it is evidence of poor monetary and fiscal policy. An *Economist* headline put it more simply, "Greedflation is a nonsense idea". This lack of foundation is not the only problem with the ACTU's proposed inquiry into unfair pricing.

In an opinion piece, Professor Fels justified his participation on the basis that companies might have "unfairly and unjustifiably increase[d] prices" and therefore a responsible government should take steps to ensure this price gouging wasn't happening. It is hardly surprising that Professor Fels would express such a view, he was the head of an institution (the ACCC) whose fundamental premise is that government is the protector and guarantor of competition in the market. This premise, too, is incorrect. Competition policy is mostly about protecting smaller companies from bigger ones, often at the expense of consumers. As markets have become more globalised, and barriers to entry (both natural and government created) have fallen, competition has increased. Governments should not stand in the way.

In fact the whole idea that the government has any business stating what a 'fair' price is for goods and services is patently absurd. The fair price for a good is the price agreed between willing buyers and sellers in an informed market. Government's role is to police fraud and misrepresentation, not competition. Not that government hasn't tried — grocery watch, fuel watch, energy watch, YourSuper, anti-dumping laws — the policy graveyard is littered with failed or mostly ineffective government policies aimed at rooting out so-called price gouging.

However, it is important to understand the bigger picture context of these claims and initiatives. The Greedflation claim, together with furious refutations of the role of wages in the current bout of inflation (something that no-one has credibly argued), seem to be about buttressing the case for wage rises linked to the level of inflation. A case which is, at least in part, government policy.

This amounts to the government seeking to apportion the pain of the necessary correction to living standards in accordance with its political priorities. But in doing so it runs a big risk: if high inflation becomes embedded in wage expectations, we could creating a disastrous, self-perpetuating inflationary cycle.

Arguably, government policy that flirts with this outcome is deeply irresponsible, hence the need to shift the debate on inflation away from wages and towards profits. But there is an even broader issue here. Underlying much of the debate around the economy, not just wages and inflation, but even the role of the Reserve Bank seems to be an attempt to effectively undo the post 70s economic settlement that assigned macroeconomic stabilisation to monetary policy and microeconomic efficiency issues to fiscal policy.

The dissidents seek to de-emphasise monetary policy, especially the role of managing inflation in monetary policy, in favour of an approach with a greater role for fiscal policy and an equal focus on maintaining full employment (or even unsustainable levels of employment). At the core, as Treasurer Jim Chalmers argued in his essay in *The Monthly* earlier this year, is the return of government to a more central role in the economy, along with bodies like the ACTU.

The ACTU inquiry will likely generate a lot of hard luck stories, and probably a fair bit of attention in support of this agenda, distracting the public from the failures of government that caused this inflation. While we should not overlook the genuine hardship the current inflationary episode has caused, too many policy initiatives are based on mistaken or misleading interpretations of economic conditions and effects.

Regardless of your ideological positioning, the policy response should be based on evidence, not superstition.

This opinion piece was originally published in 2023 by *The Canberra Times*.

Section Two: Regulation and Productivity

Robert Carling

Australia's persistent productivity slowdown is one of the defining economic challenges of our time. The chapter that follows brings together work that illuminates a central, yet too often neglected, part of this challenge: the cumulative weight of regulation and the ways in which our institutional frameworks can either enable or obstruct economic dynamism. Across these contributions runs a common message: that regulation must be disciplined, transparent, and proportionate if Australia is to restore the conditions for sustained growth.

While thoughtful regulation can serve vital public purposes, the pieces collected here show that Australia has drifted into a regime where rules accumulate without adequate scrutiny, cost-benefit analysis, or accountability. The result is a growing burden on firms, innovators, and workers. As several authors demonstrate, regulation now imposes hundreds of billions of dollars in compliance costs, stifles competition, impedes new market entrants, and slows the diffusion of new technologies. Structural productivity reform cannot succeed while this regulatory thicket remains unexamined and unreformed.

From the CORE Blueprint's emphasis on cost, opportunity, removal, and enforcement, to the proposal for regulatory budgets and sunset clauses, to the imaginative concept of a red tape trading scheme, each contribution offers mechanisms that would compel governments to prioritise, simplify, and justify regulation. Crucially, they reflect an understanding that prosperity depends not only on policy settings, but on the institutional incentives that guide officials, regulators, and ministers.

This chapter also highlights the broader implications of regulatory excess. Weak productivity growth erodes living standards, limits wage growth, and constrains the fiscal capacity required for essential public services. At a time when population growth is masking declines in output per person, and when real wages have stagnated, the stakes of restoring productivity could not be higher. The authors remind us that Australia cannot regulate its way to prosperity; it must instead create an environment in which investment, innovation, and adaptation can flourish.

Addressing Australia's Productivity Problem. CORE Blueprint to Unshackle Productivity

Jim Cox (2025)

Introduction

Australia's recent productivity performance is a serious cause for concern, with the 20-year average growth rate dropping to its lowest level in two decades. Lifting Australia's productivity growth depends on several factors including the skills and attributes of the labour force, the quality of management, the amount of public and private investment, and innovation, entrepreneurship and the rate at which new knowledge is taken up by Australian firms.

These factors are influenced but not determined by numerous government actions including taxation and spending policies, industrial relations policies, regulation, competition and energy policies. Reports from organisations such as the Productivity Commission and the OECD have identified effective policies, but their recommendations have not always been implemented.

The political economy of productivity growth presents a challenge because while the benefits of reform are diffuse, the costs are often highly concentrated on particular groups, leading to resistance. Reform is hard to achieve as governments generally focus on policies that yield visible benefits to key voting groups in the short term, rather than those offering long- term, widespread gains. However, continuing low productivity growth is likely to lead to economic outcomes that the Australian community as a whole will consider unsatisfactory.

Policies to enhance productivity growth

Sustained productivity growth requires a combination of microeconomic reform to improve efficiency and macroeconomic stability to provide a consistent environment. Key areas for policy action include:

- Labour market reform: Simplifying workplace relations and ensuring that wages are set in the context of improving productivity; facilitating the movement of labour from declining to expanding activities.
- Infrastructure: Committing to long-term infrastructure planning, particularly in energy and transport, based on rigorous cost benefit analysis that is reported to the public.
- Energy policy: Adopting a coherent technology-neutral energy policy that focusses on reliability and affordability to support businesses and households.
- Tax reform: Shifting the tax burden from economically damaging taxes (e.g. income taxes) to less distorting ones (e.g. consumption taxes) and reducing effective marginal tax rates.
- Skills and education: Improving educational outcomes and ensuring the education system delivers the skills that industry needs; emphasising skilled migration.
- Digital transformation and data policy: Facilitating the digital transformation of the economy, particularly by reforming data access and utilisation.
- Competition policy: Reinvigorating competition policy and ensuring regulators actively promote effectiveness.

A Charter of Regulatory Effectiveness (CORE)

Regulation touches every aspect of economic life, shaping the operating environment for innovation, competition and investment. Excessive and poor-quality regulation is a drag on productivity. The CORE Blueprint would enshrine in legislation principles of clear purpose, proportionality, transparency, timeliness and agility. These would apply to existing as well as new regulation. CORE would have four major components:

- Facilitate decision making by requiring regulators to be stewards of the legislation they administer.

- Streamline regulation by codifying the principles of effective regulation in legislation with emphasis on encouraging innovation and productivity growth and providing timely approvals.
- Require accountability for the effectiveness of regulatory systems from ministers and public servants through periodic reporting to Parliament.
- Provide oversight through ex-post reviews of the effectiveness of regulatory systems.

These proposals build on Australia's existing strengths – such as adaptable institutions, history of policy reform and robust democratic processes- while addressing the structural and policy barriers that have allowed productivity growth to stagnate. They recognise that productivity growth is not an end in itself, but a means of achieving higher living standards, more generous social supports, stronger environmental stewardship and greater national resilience.

Conclusion

By pursuing a coherent program of regulatory improvement, investment in human and physical capital, and a policy environment that rewards innovation, Australia can secure a more prosperous, dynamic and adaptable economy for the decades ahead. While many factors contribute to productivity growth, regulatory reform is essential to drive change. Implementing the CORE Blueprint would ensure that the cumulative burden of regulation is checked, requiring the government to prioritise and remove inefficient rules to unshackle wealth creation.

This is an edited extract of a 2025 Centre for Independent Studies research paper. The full paper can be found at https://www.cis.org.au/publication/addressing-australias-productivity-problem-core-blueprint-to-unshackle-productivity/

Productivity stakes couldn't be higher at roundtable

Gene Tunny (2025)

Treasurer Jim Chalmers promised that productivity would be the primary focus in the Albanese government's second term. That cannot come soon enough. The government's first term saw Australia enter a worrying 'per capita recession', with seven consecutive quarters of declining GDP per person. Reinforcing this concern, in the recent March quarter, GDP per capita growth again turned negative.

This is not just a statistical curiosity — it represents real declines in people's living standards. Underlying this malaise is stagnant labour productivity. Despite high levels of immigration and government spending, the economy has not been firing on all cylinders. Rather than raising our productive capacity, we have seen 'capital shallowing' — a diluting of productive capital per worker, largely due to population growth outpacing business investment.

This is not just about numbers. Productivity is the foundation of sustained wage growth, improved public services, and a higher standard of living. Without it, economic policy becomes a zero-sum game of redistribution, not wealth creation. So it is welcome that Dr Chalmers is talking up productivity — but talk must be matched by sound policy.

The story of the government's first term is discouraging. Nearly half the additional jobs created during the term were in sectors highly reliant on government spending — health care, education, social assistance such as the NDIS, and public administration. While these roles are important, they are typically lower-productivity-growth areas.

Indeed, the health and social assistance sector, although vital, is not where we expect the next wave of productivity gains. What Australia needs is a thriving private sector that can generate innovation, investment, and higher output per worker. Yet, the government's main policy settings will not achieve this.

Take industrial policy. Canberra has declared an ambition to transform Australia into a green energy superpower and rebuild domestic manufacturing. These are lofty goals, but they have been pursued through old-school, top-down interventionism — think taxpayer-funded assistance to Whyalla's steelworks, rather than addressing the underlying problem of high energy costs caused by bad policies, and targeted support to select 'priority' sectors.

The results so far are underwhelming. Manufacturing employment has barely budged. Worse, these efforts ignore one of the basic lessons of economics: letting markets allocate resources typically delivers better outcomes than government picking winners. When we direct billions in subsidies to politically favoured industries, we risk wasting taxpayer money while crowding out more productive investments.

Also troubling are the government's industrial relations reforms. Rather than supporting productivity, these policies have made our labour market more rigid and less adaptive. Changes to gig work, casual employment, and labour hire arrangements have been overly prescriptive, undermining the flexibility businesses need to operate efficiently. These reforms, championed under the banner of 'fairness', may score political points, but they deter job creation and innovation. By adding layers of compliance and reducing options for workers and employers to agree on mutually beneficial terms, the government is actively undermining its own productivity agenda.

So what should Canberra do instead? First, stop making things worse. It must resist the urge to expand government-subsidised services further or extend its interventionist policies in energy, IR, and industry.

It needs to get the NDIS under control, but it appears to lack the urgency or willingness to do so. In his Press Club address, the Treasurer celebrated that the government is on track to meet its 8% annual NDIS growth target. But this is still much faster than nominal GDP growth of 4-5% and means the NDIS will keep expanding as a share of the budget and economy, compromising productivity growth.

Second, it should look to reduce the tax burden where possible. That means curbing excessive spending and using savings to support meaningful tax reform and cuts. Indexing tax brackets to stop bracket creep would be a start. In an inflationary environment, failure to index tax thresholds means more Australians are pushed into higher tax brackets without any real increase in purchasing power. This is a hidden tax increase and a disincentive to work and invest.

Third, we must improve our education and training systems. Productivity growth depends on human capital, and we are not doing nearly enough to build it. Early screening for numeracy issues, better teacher training, and more rigorous curricula can help raise the overall quality of our workforce.

Finally, it's time to tackle the regulatory thicket that chokes business efficiency. Many regulations may have had good intentions initially but now impose costs that far outweigh any benefits. A full-scale review and rationalisation of Australia's regulatory environment is overdue. Reducing red tape would free businesses to grow, innovate and hire.

Australia has immense economic potential. We are resource-rich, educated, and globally connected. But we cannot coast on these advantages. If the Albanese government is serious about lifting productivity, it must make tough, perhaps unpopular, choices — abandoning policies that play well with vested interests but drag down growth.

The stakes could not be higher: Australia's long-term prosperity depends on it.

This opinion piece was originally published in 2025 by *The Australian.*

Red tape and Australia's economic malaise

Michael Potter (2018)

Introduction

After many years of strong economic performance, Australia is now showing signs of an 'economic malaise', characterised by sluggish productivity growth and stagnant real wages. The paper argues that a key cause of this decline is the significant increase in 'red tape' (government regulation), which restricts the economy's ability to adapt and create wealth.

Australia has become a highly regulated country, ranking poorly among developed nations for regulatory complexity.

The number of regulations and regulatory agencies has proliferated across all levels of government.

This complexity results in high compliance costs and economic distortions.

The cost of red tape

The overall cost of regulation has two components:

1. Compliance costs: The direct costs (time and money) of complying with regulations, estimated at over $200 billion annually.

2. Economic costs, or deadweight losses: The indirect costs from regulations preventing efficient resource allocation, thus lowering productivity and economic growth. The total economic cost is likely much higher than the direct compliance costs

Red tape, dynamism and productivity

Excessive regulation hinders economic dynamism and is a primary cause of Australia's productivity slowdown and stagnant real wages.

- Dynamism is the process of economic adaptation and creative destruction, where new, more productive firms displace older, less efficient ones.
- Red tape makes it harder for new firms to enter the market and for existing firms to innovate, thereby reducing this crucial churn and growth.

The problem with regulation

There are three major issues with the volume and quality of regulation:

1. Quantity: The sheer volume of new regulations makes it impossible for businesses to keep up, leading to high compliance costs.
2. Quality: Regulations are often poorly designed, failing to meet their stated objectives while causing significant unintended negative consequences.
3. Lack of Sunset Clauses: Regulations rarely expire, creating a cumulative burden over time.

Regulatory failure

The current system exhibits regulatory failure, as it fails to balance the benefits of regulation with its costs.

- Common responses are 'one-in, one-out' or 'two-for-one' rules, which attempt to control the volume of new regulations but have generally failed in practice.
- Competition policy is also being eroded by the growth of regulation.

Recommendations

To combat regulatory inertia and stimulate the economy, the paper recommends a sweeping response to regulation reduction, including:

Regulatory Budgets: Introducing 'regulatory budgets' that assign an explicit dollar cost to every regulation. This forces governments to publicly account for regulatory costs and make trade-offs, like those made in standard financial budgets.

Regulatory Sunset: Establishing a statutory rule that all existing and future regulations automatically expire (sunset) after a fixed period, such as 5 or 7 years, unless actively reviewed and renewed by parliament.

Institutional Reform: Creating an independent Office of Regulatory Reduction to enforce regulatory budgets, administer sunset clauses, and hold regulators accountable.

Regulatory Benchmarks: Using benchmarks (such as the *Doing Business* rankings) to set clear targets for improvement in regulatory performance.

Fixing incentives: reintroduce payments to states to encourage reform, and address the disincentives for reform caused by the way money is distributed to the states.

Remove bias towards regulation: ensure the burden of proof is on those wishing to add new regulations, or retain existing regulations after they have sunsetted.

This is an edited extract of a 2018 Centre for Independent Studies research paper. The full paper can be found at https://www.cis.org.au/publication/red-tape-and-australias-economic-malaise/

Towards a Red Tape Trading Scheme: Treating excessive bureaucracy as just another kind of pollution

Oliver Marc Hartwich (2010)

Introduction

For many years now, trading schemes have been used as mechanisms to reduce environmental pollution. The principal idea behind such schemes is that they allow emissions to be cut where it is least costly. A similar idea could be applied in the area of better regulation. Although in some areas regulation may be desirable or necessary, there are regulatory costs associated with it. The challenge for politicians and regulators is to keep these costs to a minimum. A trading scheme for regulatory costs could help achieve this.

The basic idea behind such a trading scheme is borrowed from trading schemes for environmental pollutions. After an initial stock-take of regulatory costs (the bureaucracy costs resulting from regulation), certificates are issued to government departments and agencies. These certificates give them the right to impose regulatory costs on business. In the next step, the total amount of certificates is cut below the initial level. Government departments will then have to cut the regulatory costs they impose; if they fail to achieve these cuts, they have to purchase certificates from other departments.

Such a trading scheme for regulatory costs would ensure that regulatory costs are removed where their removal is easiest. Regulators would be free to creatively simplify regulations and reduce their burden on society. In order to make a regulatory cost trading scheme work, a precise measurement of existing regulatory costs is necessary. Even without a trading scheme, it would still be desirable to measure these costs because we can only speculate the current costs of red tape to the Australian economy.

In recent years, the Dutch have pioneered a system to measure regulatory burdens. The Standard Cost Model, which was pioneered by the the former Dutch Advisory Board on Administrative Burden — (ACTAL, or *Adviescollege toetsing administratieve lasten*) — measures regulatory burdens. It identifies the amount of time necessary to comply with a specific regulation and then calculates how much this would cost. This figure is then multiplied by the number of businesses affected by the regulation, which delivers the total regulatory burden associated with this particular measure. By measuring red tape through the Standard Cost Model, the Dutch have been able to issue targets for reducing these burdens. The Dutch model has been so successful that other countries have adopted it. The Dutch approach is a good first step in dealing with regulatory burdens, and if it is applied in combination with a trading scheme for regulatory burdens it could unleash even greater creativity in identifying ways to cut red tape where it is least needed.

The scheme would start with an initial stock-take of regulatory costs, after which certificates would be issued to government departments, granting them the right to impose these costs on business. The total amount of certificates would then be cut below the initial level, forcing departments to either reduce the regulatory costs they impose or purchase certificates from other departments that have been more successful at cutting red tape. This trading mechanism would reward departments that excel at reducing burdens with extra funds, while those who fail would feel the pinch in their allocated budgets. The advantage of any trading scheme is that it uses dispersed knowledge, allowing practitioners (bureaucrats) closest to the source of the burden to decide the most effective way to cut it.

To make this scheme work, a precise measurement of existing regulatory costs is necessary. The report recommends adopting the Standard Cost Model, pioneered by the Dutch ACTAL authority. This model measures administrative burdens by identifying the time necessary to comply with a regulation, calculating the cost of that time, and multiplying the result by the number of businesses affected. The Dutch model has been successful, enabling the government to issue and achieve targets for reducing administrative burdens. The report argues that combining the Dutch approach with a trading scheme could unleash even greater creativity in cutting red tape.

Basics of regulatory trading explained

Environmental trading schemes are designed to reduce total emissions by capping the amount of emissions below current levels. The market mechanism then allows participants to decide by how much each individual cuts emissions, ensuring that reductions occur where they are cheapest. To transpose this to regulation, the 'players' are identified as the government departments. The government would treat each department as an individual polluter. After measuring the total regulatory burden, the government would set a reduction target (e.g., 5% in one year) and cap the total sum of burdens. Departments would receive Red Tape Certificates representing their allowed pollution.

The cap-and-trade mechanism would work similarly to an emissions trading scheme, but the trade would occur between government departments. Departments that exceed their reduction target can sell their excess certificates to departments that fall short. This provides an incentive to reduce red tape and a financial punishment for failing to do so, as only allocated funds can be used to buy certificates. The crucial advantage is that bureaucrats are most aware of the burdens they place on the public and are best placed to estimate the potential for reductions.

Going Dutch about measuring red tape

The successful operation of a trading scheme depends on getting the initial measurement right. Currently, only disparate rough estimates of regulatory costs to the Australian economy are available, making a systematic evaluation highly desirable. The Dutch Standard Cost Model (SCM) provides the necessary systematic measurement. The SCM focuses only on a regulation's administrative costs (compliance costs), not its policy goals or merits. The basic formula is: Price x Time x Quantity. Price equals the hourly wage plus administrative overheads; Time is the time needed to deal with the regulation; and Quantity is the number of units and the frequency of compliance.

The Dutch body, ACTAL, was founded to estimate total administrative costs and monitor reductions. Its first measurement in 2002 was €16.2 billion. The government set, and achieved, an initial 25% reduction target over five years. ACTAL's success stems from its simplicity and narrow focus—it only quantifies the bureaucracy created by regulation, such as form-filling and applying for licences.

Measuring red tape needs an independent home

ACTAL's success is due to its independence, which ensures its advice has political weight. In Australia, the report suggests the Productivity Commission would be the most suitable institutional home, given its focus on economic efficiency and independence, making it closer to ACTAL than the Commonwealth government's Office of Best Practice Regulation (OBPR).

The Productivity Commission's mandate should be extended to include measuring administrative burdens via the Standard Cost Model and routinely consulting on new legislation's effect on administrative costs. Furthermore, it would be logical to put the Productivity Commission in charge of organising the market for Red Tape Certificates between government departments, as it would possess all the necessary cost information.

How would Red Tape Trading work in practice?

The scheme would begin with the Productivity Commission establishing a monitoring system and measuring the existing regulatory burdens for each department, which would serve as the baseline. The government would then set an overall percentage reduction target that is applied across the board to all departments to avoid bargaining for special concessions.

It may be advantageous to set targets for shorter periods, such as the fiscal year, synchronising the regulatory burdens budget (certificates) with the fiscal budget process. For example, a 5% reduction would mean departments receive certificates worth 95% of the base year's pollution. Departments would then have to reduce their burdens or buy certificates from more successful departments on the market organised by the Productivity Commission. The department head should be free to decide how to spend the additional revenue from trading, strengthening the incentive for reduction.

Red Tape Trading and the Standard Cost Model: the future of regulatory reform?

While the trading scheme idea is a thought experiment, administrative burdens share characteristics with other pollutants as wasteful by-products. An across-the-board cut would allow the pitfall of compensating polluters, often seen in environmental schemes, to be avoided, as it would be politically difficult for ministers to argue for imposing greater bureaucratic burdens.

The key to success lies in the simplicity of the Standard Cost Model and the independence of the monitoring body (ACTAL/Productivity Commission). Even just an official estimate of total regulatory burdens would be progress; an independently monitored, fractionally reduced annual burden would be better; and a scheme informed by pollution reduction experiences could be a promising new approach for regulatory reform.

This is an edited extract of a 2010 Centre for Independent Studies research paper. The full paper can be found at https://www.cis.org.au/publication/towards-a-red-tape-trading-scheme-treating-excessive-bureaucracy-as-just-another-kind-of-pollution/

Productivity Commission piles in to Labor's schizophrenic war on big business

Michael Stutchbury (2025)

Industry Minister Tim Ayres rightly says that Australia is in competition for global capital as he throws taxpayer money at propping up old steel mills and smelters. Yet, at the same time, the Productivity Commission calls for an even heavier tax burden on the big companies that drive most of the new business investment needed to revive Australia's stalled productivity.

And so the traditionally independent PC has joined Labor's schizophrenic war on big business. Under its plan, Australia's 500 biggest firms — those with annual revenue above $1 billion — would continue to pay the 30 per cent company tax rate that the PC agrees has become internationally uncompetitive.

These big companies would be further hit by the 'incentive' of a new 5% net cash flow tax that supposedly would target their excess profits and reward extra investment spending. This would aim to create 'a more dynamic and resilient economy': the PC even cites one of Jim Chalmers' favourite economists, capitalist critic Marianna Mazzucato, in second guessing what company tax policy would be 'implementable' for the Albanese government.

The PC points to a fall in both the birth rate of new firms and the death rate of old firms as evidence of weaker creative destruction. Less economic dynamism in turn means that "large parts of our economy are not working" the way they should. "In many sectors a small number of big firms exercise market power to the detriment of consumers," the PC complains.

Its commissioned economic modelling makes the frankly unbelievable claim that 54% of Australia's company tax base takes the form of 'economic rents', up from 31% before the pandemic. It's a utopia for oligopoly capitalists, presumably led by the big miners, the big banks, the big two supermarket chains and the likes of CSL and Wesfarmers' Bunnings. 'Rents' are the economists' label for profits above the 'normal' returns that would be generated by a market in which firms vigorously compete against each other. Theoretically, such excess profits could be taxed more heavily without prompting firms to cut back their investment in new capacity.

Labor is instinctively drawn to this narrative of big companies exploiting their market power, ripping off consumers and fuelling inflation. Egged on by the Nationals, the Coalition has become even more anti big-business and populist at times. Treasurer Chalmers last year pointed to unbelievable claims of a "near doubling" of market concentration to justify giving the Australian Competition and Consumer Commission tougher powers to block corporate mergers. Anthony Albanese began his last election campaign promising heavy fines against "price gouging" by Woolworths and Coles: defined as when they "take the piss" against their customers.

But it is devilishly difficult to measure 'rents' in any sensible way, as Sinclair Davidson explains in a Centre for Independent Studies analysis of the PC's proposed net cash flow tax. Gas exporters reasonably will seek much more than the 10-year government bond yield before risking tens of billions of dollars on the volatile global energy market and amid political hazards that could retrospectively force them to divert sales to the domestic market.

The prime minister's claims of supermarket price gouging came as a one-year ACCC study found no evidence of such profiteering. Australian supermarkets even increased grocery prices less than in most other developed economies. Until now, the PC typically dismissed attempts to blame corporate power for any dulling of economic dynamism.

In Australia, sectors such as banking, airlines, supermarkets and cement appear dominated by a small number of big firms. But just two years ago, the PC found most industries "are not highly concentrated". And oligopolists can still compete vigorously: as in what previous PC analysis has described as Australia's "highly competitive" supermarket sector.

Competition from mortgage brokers, global big tech payment providers and the disruptive entry of Macquarie has squeezed big bank home lending margins. Yes, the big iron ore exporters have been well-rewarded for taking the now-rising risk on China — but their hefty profits don't hurt Australian consumers. And digital technology has left Australia more exposed than ever to global competition: start with the entry of Amazon, the decline of department stores and the smashing of traditional media. The dismantling of the tariff wall exposed car makers to so much import competition that they shut up shop here.

And the related PC proposal to cut the company tax rate to 20% for smaller companies that earn less than $1 billion in annual revenue wouldn't offset the investment hit from taxing big companies more. It's big business that mostly drives the economy's productive capacity. The top 1% of firms account for about one-half of all non-mining capital investment in Australia, according to Reserve Bank research.

As Industry Minister Ayres is discovering, globally focused big companies have the option of moving production to where tax rates, energy costs, labour regulation and other costs are less onerous than here. Business investment has been crowded out by the expansion of the less-productive care economy and strangled by what the PC calls the "ever growing burden of regulation". Ironically, it is this costly red tape and compliance burden that often makes it harder for new firms to challenge more-established rivals.

This opinion piece was originally published in 2025 by the *Australian Financial Review.*

Section Three: Government Spending

Robert Carling

This chapter examines one of the most enduring and least resolved issues in modern political economy: the relentless growth of government. Across more than a century, advanced economies — Australia among them — have experienced a spasmodic expansion in public spending, public employment, taxation, and state intervention. Yet this fundamental transformation of the relationship between citizens and the state rarely receives the scrutiny it deserves. The work collected here helps to fill that gap, offering a rigorous and historically informed exploration of why government grows, what drives its contemporary acceleration, and what the consequences will be if current trends continue unchecked. The authors approach the question from multiple angles — economic, demographic, institutional and theoretical — and together they reveal a picture far more complex than any single narrative can explain.

Crises have had lasting ratchet effects; ageing populations have increased the demand for health and social services; changes in the way democracy works have encouraged expansion of government spending; and cultural shifts have fostered a deepening reliance on government provision. In the Australian context, the emergence and rapid growth of social programs — from Medicare to the NDIS — have entrenched expectations that would have been unthinkable only a few decades ago. A recurring theme in this chapter is the widening gap between the scale of government and the institutional constraints that once disciplined it. As several contributors note, Australia's public spending reflects not just new commitments but a culture of political incentives that rewards expansion and punishes restraint. Off-budget financing, opaque investment vehicles and the proliferation of policy-driven lending further weaken transparency and accountability. The result is a fiscal trajectory that is neither sustainable nor consistent with long-term productivity growth.

The chapter also highlights the profound economic and social costs of this shift. Beyond a certain point, government expansion slows productivity, erodes private investment, raises taxes and debt, and entrenches a dependency that corrodes civil society. The authors argue, convincingly, that Australia is approaching that point. Rising expenditure in the care economy, growing interest burdens, and escalating commitments in defence, infrastructure and welfare will strain future budgets, limit flexibility, and weaken the country's capacity to respond to crises. The need for reform is urgent. Yet these essays do more than diagnose the problem. They outline institutional and policy reforms — from expenditure restraint and program reviews to enhanced fiscal transparency and rules-based discipline — that could help restore balance.

Why Does Government Grow?

Stephen Kirchner (2011)

Executive Summary

Government size has increased substantially across developed countries since 1900. Australia's government remains relatively small by international standards but shares this upward trend. Theories explaining government growth provide only partial insights and are often difficult to distinguish empirically. While large government is typically linked with weaker economic growth, the relationship is complex: economic development can increase demand for government without direct causality, and governments can become more efficient as they expand. Classical liberals, while concerned about inefficiency and threats to civil society, may inadvertently encourage government growth through policies that improve efficiency and revenue capacity. A broader defence of limited government requires understanding the powerful forces driving this expansion.

Introduction

Government has grown markedly since the early twentieth century. Australia's spending remains modest compared to other nations, yet it too has experienced persistent expansion. Despite this, the issue receives little scrutiny. Treasury projections foresee spending growth continuing, with fiscal pressures likely to increase. Former Treasury Secretary Ken Henry predicted that tax revenues would eventually need to expand to meet community demand for public services, assuming continued demand-driven growth in government.

Explanations for this growth are incomplete and often overlapping.

Although a negative correlation exists between government size and economic growth, causation is uncertain. Governments may expand in ways that increase efficiency, softening expected negative impacts. Classical liberals, focusing narrowly on efficiency, have sometimes facilitated larger, more sustainable governments. A broader institutional approach is needed to restrain government growth.

Growth in the Size of Government

Historical data show that government's share of economic output has generally increased since the late seventeenth century, with major wars having a ratchet effect that permanently raised spending levels. A temporary decline occurred in the nineteenth century due to peace and globalisation, but from 1900 onwards — spurred by world wars, depression, and the welfare state — growth resumed. Studies suggest that many modern governments exceeded their efficient size around the 1960s.

Growth in the Size of Australian Government

Australian data show a long-term rise in taxation as a share of GDP from around 2% in 1850 to about 30% by the 2000s. Economic performance remained strong even when government was small. Other indicators of government size include legislative activity, which has expanded sharply since Federation.

- In 1907, only 12 Acts were passed; by 1992, 282 Acts were enacted.
- The number of legislative pages has grown dramatically since the 1970s, increasing legal complexity.
- The number of federal ministers has risen from 7 in 1901 to 42 today, with over 230 federal agencies now in operation.

These measures demonstrate the steady expansion of both the size and scope of Australian government, as well as centralisation of power at the federal level.

Theories of Government Growth

The main theoretical explanations for growth can be examined under Buchanan's taxonomy, dividing them into citizen-over-state and state-over-citizen models, along with deterministic and ideological perspectives.

Buchanan's Taxonomy

The citizen-over-state model sees government expansion as demand-driven and welfare-enhancing; the state-over-citizen model sees it as supply-driven and self-serving. Other theories introduce external or cultural drivers.

Citizen-over-state

Wagner's Law argues that as societies become richer, industrialised, and more urbanised, citizens demand more public services, leading to higher public spending. Empirical tests yield mixed results, but a long-term relationship between economic development and government expansion is evident.

Median-voter and rational-choice theories suggest government grows through voter preferences for redistribution rather than public goods. Competitive politics can act like a market, aggregating voter preferences efficiently, though these models rely on restrictive assumptions.

State-over-citizen

In this view, government expands through self-interest or coercion.

- Oppenheimer and Olson depict the state as predatory, serving entrenched interests.

    Brennan and Buchanan's "Leviathan" model sees government as a revenue-maximising entity constrained by constitutions and federal systems. Empirical evidence suggests that governments may have exceeded their economically optimal size—around 20–23% of GDP. Technological and social changes, such as greater female labour participation, have expanded the taxable base, easing fiscal constraints and sustaining larger government. Reforms making tax systems more efficient may paradoxically allow government to grow further by reducing resistance to expansion.

Deterministic and Path Dependency Theories

These explanations attribute growth to external structural factors:

- Demography: Ageing populations increase demand for public health and pensions.
- Technology: Improvements in communication and transport extend government reach.
- Baumol's Disease: Low productivity growth in public services raises their cost share.
- Globalisation: While increasing competition might limit government size, small open economies often expand welfare to shield citizens from external shocks.
- Ratchet Effect: Wars and crises cause lasting increases in government spending.

Each factor is bounded, suggesting government cannot grow indefinitely, but all contribute to persistent expansion.

Zeitgeist Explanations

These theories stress the role of ideas and ideology. Shifts from nineteenth-century liberalism to twentieth-century collectivism paralleled rising government size. However, ideology may follow rather than cause these changes. Even the classical liberal revival of the late twentieth century failed to halt government expansion, suggesting that intellectual trends alone are insufficient. Hayek and Caplan both emphasise the need for sustained public engagement by liberals to counter persistent "rational irrationality" favouring intervention.

Conclusion

Government has grown steadily across developed economies for over a century, and Australia is no exception. Multiple interacting forces—economic, political, demographic, and ideological—drive this process, making any single "grand explanation" elusive. While many governments have likely exceeded their efficient size, the limits of expansion remain uncertain.

The concern is less the absolute size of government than the weakening of constitutional and institutional constraints that once contained it. As markets and societies become more complex, the need for clear limits and decentralised decision-making grows. To effectively argue for limited government, classical liberals must pair efficiency arguments with advocacy for rules and institutions that restrain the state's long-term expansion.

This is an edited extract of a 2011 Centre for Independent Studies research paper. The full paper can be found at https://www.cis.org.au/publication/why-does-government-grow/

Australia's Future Fiscal Shock

Robert Carling (2012)

Executive Summary

Australia's governments focus too narrowly on short-term budget balance while neglecting long-term fiscal pressures. Under current policies, public spending could exceed 40% of GDP within decades, driven by new spending commitments and population ageing. Without corrective action, this would require significantly higher taxation or borrowing. The financial crises in Europe and the United States highlight the risks of large government and sustained fiscal deficits. Australia still has time to act, but new programs such as the NDIS, aged care reforms, and education funding are expanding future obligations. Governments must restrain new spending, offset any new commitments with savings, and increase transparency around long-term fiscal sustainability.

Introduction

Australia's public finances face mounting long-term pressures. Although budgets are close to balance, many expensive policy ideas are being developed with costs beyond the four-year forward estimates. The global financial crisis underscored how sustained high spending levels contributed to debt crises in advanced economies. Australia's relatively low debt and moderate tax burden give a misleading impression of fiscal strength. Intergenerational reports (IGRs) from the Commonwealth and states project that current policies will produce unsustainable fiscal gaps in coming decades. Radical reform of public financial management is needed to maintain sustainability.

What's Wrong with Big Government?

Large governments impose heavy tax and debt burdens that reduce economic efficiency and flexibility. Though the 2008 financial crisis began in private markets, it exposed the fiscal vulnerability of countries with long-standing high public expenditure. Research suggests that beyond roughly 30% of GDP, government spending becomes economically inefficient. With total public expenditure near 36% of GDP, Australia must proceed carefully. Excessive public debt, typically above 90% of GDP, is linked to slower economic growth and greater risk of sovereign default. While Australia's debt remains modest, its overall debt — including household and external borrowing — is high enough to justify caution.

Australia's Government Sector in Perspective

Among OECD countries, Australia's total public sector—at around 36% of GDP—is small only compared with Europe's very large governments, many exceeding 50% of GDP. Australia's relatively lean age pension system and means-tested benefits have restrained spending growth, unlike Europe's universal and contributory welfare models. However, pressures from ageing, health, and social programs could expand spending towards European levels. Public debt remains low, but future borrowing to fund new programs could add to overall debt risks. If historical trends persist, government spending could exceed 40% of GDP within decades.

Long-Term Growth of Government Spending

Government spending has grown steadily since World War II, rising from less than 20% of GDP to around 36% today. Most of this increase comes from new policies rather than the automatic growth of existing programs. Between 2000 and 2010, three-quarters of Commonwealth spending growth resulted from new initiatives. Without such new programs, real spending growth would have been about 1% per year rather than 4%. To contain future expansion, governments must curb their appetite for new initiatives or find real savings to offset them—something that current political incentives discourage.

2050: A Fiscal Odyssey

The 2010 Commonwealth Intergenerational Report projected that, under existing policies, expenditure would rise to above 40% of GDP by 2050, creating a fiscal gap of around 2.75% of GDP. If not addressed early, this gap will lead to higher debt and interest payments, pushing total spending into the mid-40% range. State-level projections show similar unsustainability. These estimates understate risks because they exclude new policies adopted since 2010. Without action, Australia faces the same long-term fiscal deterioration experienced by many advanced economies.

New Pressures for Bigger Government

Despite warnings, governments continue to introduce costly new programs. Since 2010, new commitments include:

- National Disability Insurance Scheme (NDIS) – projected cost up to $22 billion per year.
- National Injury Insurance Scheme (NIIS) – around $1 billion.
- Superannuation and low-income tax changes – costing $5 billion in lost revenue.
- Community sector pay increases, child care subsidies, aged care reforms, and education funding (Gonski) – billions more in annual costs.
- Dental care, paid parental leave, and border protection – additional major outlays.

These and similar commitments could add around $28 billion per year (2% of GDP) to public spending by 2020. Combined with demographic pressures, this would raise government spending to about 43–45% of GDP by 2050.

Implications and Remedies

Unchecked, these trends will produce much higher tax or debt burdens. To avoid this, governments should:

- Limit new programs and improve the efficiency of existing spending.

- Require new expenditure to be offset by savings elsewhere.
- Conduct comprehensive audits to rebase budgets at lower spending levels.
- Use user charges more widely to align service costs with benefits.

If spending restraint fails, tax revenue would need to rise from around 27–30% of GDP to nearly 40%, greatly increasing economic costs. Political and community expectations must adjust to the reality of limited resources.

Transparency and Credibility

Improved transparency would strengthen fiscal discipline. Current four-year forward estimates are easily manipulated and insufficient for long-term management. Carling recommends:

- Annual Fiscal Sustainability Updates reporting the long-term impact of policy decisions.
- Coordination of Commonwealth and state IGRs to create a unified national outlook.
- Possible oversight by an independent fiscal authority or the Productivity Commission.
- Extending forward estimates to 10 years to better align with intergenerational projections.

Such measures would hold governments accountable for policies that affect fiscal sustainability beyond the immediate budget cycle.

Summary and Conclusion

The fiscal crises in Europe and North America reveal the dangers of prolonged government expansion and weak budget discipline. Although Australia's position remains relatively strong, the trajectory of spending and new commitments risks leading to the same outcome — high taxes, debt, and slower growth. If spending continues to rise as it has over the past 40 years, the public sector could reach 45–50% of GDP by 2050. The lesson is clear: governments must act now to curb spending, reform institutions for long-term discipline, and prevent a future fiscal shock.

This is an edited extract of a 2012 Centre for Independent Studies research paper. The full paper can be found at https://www.cis.org.au/publication/australias-future-fiscal-shock-2/

Government spending needs reform before taxes

Robert Carling (2024)

I would like a dollar for every time I've read how much the Australian economy needs tax reform. Sure, it does — but what about the growth and inefficiency of government expenditure that's driving up the tax burden in the first place? What about expenditure reform?

Advocates of tax reform often present it as a restructuring of the tax system, perhaps with a dash of simplification thrown into the mix. But some have also been candid enough to reveal their underlying objective — to increase overall tax revenue to satisfy the growing financing demands of government expenditure. This is not revenue-neutral or tax-cutting reform such as we have seen in the past, but tax-increasing reform.

Before even considering going down that path, we need government expenditure reform in order to improve efficiency and effectiveness of programs, rationalise roles and responsibilities of different tiers of government, and relieve the upward pressure of spending growth on taxation and borrowing. The recently announced changes to aged care funding and the NDIS are examples of what expenditure reform should look like, at least qualitatively.

Whether either set of changes goes far enough in relieving the budgetary pressures from these programs is another matter. The aged care reforms merely lower the spending growth rate from 5.7% to 5.2% a year, while the NDIS changes aim to reduce growth in the cost of that program to

8% — which is still very high. But the reforms are to be welcomed for tackling two of the big pressure points on the federal budget and for making permanent structural changes that will lead to increasing savings over time.

Political sustainability is secured by grandfathering existing beneficiaries and by securing the Opposition's support. This takes the political heat out of these issues, at least for one election ahead. This doesn't mean that all reform can be bipartisan. The logical end to that would be a German style 'grand coalition' government of Labor, Liberal and the Nationals — which has only helped Europe's largest nation and economy reclaim the 'sick man of Europe' title. The major parties should stick to their principles and give the voters a genuine choice. On many topics this means bipartisanship is impossible.

A lack of bipartisanship, however, doesn't let the elected government off the hook of managing its spending responsibly and devising and implementing needed reforms. Our federal, state and territory governments are not living up to that responsibility. They are best at thinking up new ways to spend more — and without giving much attention to whether the benefits justify the costs.

Too often the 'more' is just added to existing program costs with no attempt to review those programs for inefficiencies, ineffectiveness and potential savings. One route to expenditure reform is to review everything at once as the basis for a 'horror budget'. This works only when there is an economic crisis or a newly elected government with a lot of political capital.

Even then, it didn't work for the newly elected Abbott government in 2013, which launched a whole-of-government review by an appointed commission of audit. That exercise was notable for all it failed to achieve — not because there was anything wrong with the commission's recommendations, but because it started a political firestorm the government could not contain.

The omnibus approach probably belongs to a bygone era when special interest groups were less well organised and resourced, social media was unheard of, and governments could usually rely on the Senate to pass their legislation. An alternative to the omnibus approach is a methodical program-by-program review of all areas of government spending, including the overlap between the federal and state/territory governments.

The institutional structure to support this exists, including the Productivity Commission and the new Australian Centre for Evaluation within the Treasury. It shouldn't take a Royal Commission to set the scene for a review in any program, such as was the case with aged care. And the fact that a methodical, program-by-program approach will take time doesn't matter.

The problem with it is of a different kind. It is that, more often than not, the focus is not on efficiency, effectiveness, value for money and restraint, but on pathbreaking social reformism with a huge price tag. That is how the poorly designed NDIS (for example) came about in the first place, and we see the same mentality alive and well now in areas such as childcare, education and demands to extend Medicare to dental services.

If the attachment to collectivist models, government intervention and social engineering prevails, the outlook for more of what we have just seen in the aged care reform package is not promising.

This opinion piece was originally published in 2024 by *the Spectator*.

Leviathan on the Rampage

Robert Carling (2025)

Executive Summary

Government spending in Australia has risen to almost 39% of GDP — up from around 34–35% before the 2008 Global Financial Crisis — creating growing fiscal, economic and social risks. At the Commonwealth level, spending has increased from about 25% of GDP to above 27%. Since 2012–13, real per capita Commonwealth expenditure has grown by 1.8% annually, far outpacing productivity and GDP growth. A dozen fast-growing programs — mainly in social and 'care' sectors, defence and debt interest — now absorb half of the federal budget.

This pattern reflects a deepening culture of dependency and entitlement that drives expectations for continual government expansion. Administrative costs have risen sharply since the pandemic, and while forward estimates suggest moderation, this is implausible given the many fiscal pressures ahead. Without reform, Australia risks drifting towards European-style welfare statism. Expenditure restraint is as essential as tax reform for maintaining economic vitality and fiscal sustainability.

Introduction

The growth of government expenditure is a long-standing trend that has accelerated over the past five years. Key recent drivers include the pandemic, inflation, new defence commitments, and promises made in the 2025 election campaign. The report examines Commonwealth expenditure since 2012–13 — the period marking the start of major social programs such as the NDIS — and analyses its causes, consequences and likely trajectory. The author argues that without decisive spending restraint, Australia will move toward a European-sized welfare state.

A Culture of Dependency

A pervasive dependency culture underpins government growth. Citizens increasingly expect support and resist its withdrawal, believing others will pay. Lobby groups and welfare-sector organisations reinforce this dynamic, while politicians cater to it for electoral gain.

Historically, Australia has relied on government intervention since colonial times, and though once mitigated by targeted welfare and private superannuation, universal in-kind programs like Medicare, the NDIS and childcare have entrenched expectations of 'free' services. This entitlement mentality is now evident in political campaigns and public attitudes that prioritise personal benefit over fiscal responsibility.

As more Australians rely on government employment or welfare, the electorate itself becomes a constituency for big government. The paper labels this 'voting for a living' — a shift from creating value in the market to seeking income via state redistribution.

The Economic and Social Harm from Government Spending Growth

While inflation has recently drawn attention to excessive public spending, the broader concern lies in its long-term effects. Beyond a certain level, marginal benefits from extra spending diminish while marginal costs rise through higher taxes and debt.

Large governments crowd out private investment and distort resource allocation, leading to weaker productivity and slower growth. Socially, dependence on government corrodes self-reliance, philanthropy, and civic initiative, while fostering rent-seeking and political lobbying. With over 30% of the workforce employed in public or publicly funded sectors, and more than half of voters reliant on government income, political resistance to fiscal restraint is formidable.

Putting the Trump Administration's Government Efficiency Drive into Perspective

The new US administration's efficiency campaign, led by Elon Musk, highlights the global challenge of restraining public spending. Its limited success illustrates that targeting administrative costs alone cannot restore fiscal balance. The same lesson applies to Australia: while trimming bureaucracy is necessary, the main drivers of fiscal expansion are social transfers, subsidies and interest payments.

National Government Expenditure

Total government expenditure in Australia has risen from around 34–35% of GDP before the GFC to 38–39% today. Commonwealth expenditure accounts for most of this increase, having grown from 24–25% to 27–28% of GDP.

Since 1999–2000, total government spending has quadrupled in nominal terms and more than doubled in real terms. Real per capita government spending has increased by 1.9% a year — faster than productivity growth. The long-term upward trend, dating back to the 1970s, places the size of Australia's total public sector at mid-range among advanced economies once outliers like France are excluded.

Focus on the Commonwealth Government

From 2012–13 to 2024–25, Commonwealth spending rose from 25% to 27.6% of GDP, growing 6% annually in nominal terms and 3.3% in real terms — faster than GDP. Growth was moderate until 2018–19, surged during the pandemic, and has accelerated again since 2022–23. Current spending levels represent a structural increase of around 2–3% of GDP, or $55 billion annually, above pre-2013 norms.

Lifting the Lid on Fast-Growing Expenditure Programmes

A small set of fast-growing programs — including the NDIS, aged care, education, health, defence, and debt interest — has driven most of the growth. These items grew at an average of 9% a year since 2012–13, compared with 3.9% for all others.

The NDIS dominates this list, alongside Medicare, the PBS, schools, hospitals, aged care, childcare and transport. Together, these programs now consume nearly half of all Commonwealth expenditure and will account for more than 80% of new spending growth to 2028–29.

Impact of the Covid-19 Pandemic

Pandemic spending totalled over $300 billion and permanently increased debt service costs by about $10 billion a year. Beyond this, the crisis normalised fiscal profligacy: governments and voters alike became more tolerant of deficits and debt. As with the GFC, pandemic-era spending lifted the baseline of government expenditure to a permanently higher level.

How Much Have Departmental Running Costs Contributed?

Public service costs remained contained until 2021, then accelerated sharply under the current government. APS employment rose by 38,000 between 2021 and 2024, and employee expenses grew 7.8% annually in that period. Combined administrative costs (staff and operations) have increased 6% annually since 2021–22.

Meanwhile, public sector and government-funded employment in health, education and social services now comprises over 31% of the workforce, reflecting a structural shift toward the labour-intensive 'care economy'.

Interpreting Trends

Official forward estimates assume spending growth will slow markedly after 2024–25, but this is doubtful. Planned slowdowns in NDIS, schools and other areas are politically implausible. Meanwhile, rising interest payments will accelerate overall growth. The likely outcome is a sustained or even higher spending-to-GDP ratio rather than the projected decline.

Future Pressure Points – More of the Same

Key pressure areas include:

- **Defence:** likely to rise beyond 3% of GDP due to AUKUS and geopolitical risks.
- **NDIS:** growth targeted to slow to 8% annually, but cost control remains doubtful.
- **Schools and Health:** recurrent demands for more funding despite poor outcomes.
- **Aged Care, Child Care, and Wages:** expansionary pressures continue, with new Commonwealth commitments to subsidise wage rises.
- **Infrastructure:** Commonwealth outlays for transport have more than tripled since 2012–13 and remain vulnerable to cost blowouts.

Together, these factors make further expenditure increases almost inevitable without policy intervention.

'Off-Budget' Government Expenditure

Governments increasingly use 'off-budget' financing — loans and investments classed as 'financial assets for policy purposes' — to conceal real spending. These transactions, covering schemes such as the NBN, Snowy Hydro and green finance, add roughly $104 billion to cash outlays over five years, inflating debt while improving only the appearance of fiscal discipline.

How Can Leviathan Be Tamed?

Fiscal consolidation does not require nominal cuts but credible restraint below GDP growth. Essential steps include:

- Rolling reviews of major programs to reduce cost growth and improve efficiency.
- Offsetting all new spending with savings elsewhere.
- Fiscal rules to limit per capita expenditure growth.

- Freezing or reducing public service numbers.

Achieving structural balance by 2029–30 would mirror successful consolidations of the 1980s and 1990s. Without such reform, deficits, debt and taxes will inexorably rise.

Conclusion

Australia's government has expanded steadily for decades, with social programs, defence, and administrative costs driving the latest surge. The pandemic entrenched higher spending levels, and projected moderation lacks credibility. Expenditure reform is now as critical as tax reform to safeguard fiscal health and productivity.

Without a deliberate effort to 'tame Leviathan', Australia faces a future of entrenched dependency, rising debt, and diminished economic vitality.

This is an edited extract of a 2025 Centre for Independent Studies research paper. The full paper can be found at https://www.cis.org.au/publication/leviathan-on-the-rampage-how-the-growth-of-government-is-draining-australias-economic-vitality/

Government's spending surge a threat to productivity

Robert Carling and Simon Cowan (2025)

It has been clear for some time that the Treasurer is sympathetic to calls for an expanded role for government. His much-cited essay on the future of capitalism outlined a vision of government returning to the centre of the economy, using taxpayer funds to direct and shape economic priorities. This is a bad idea; both on its merits, and in terms of its negative impact on productivity.

The fact is government has been steadily growing in both its expenditure and regulatory dimensions for years now and each of these are a drain on productivity. Focusing on expenditure, a full tally for all levels of government shows expenditure at 38.3% of GDP in 2023-24 and it is likely to have been higher in 2024-25, perhaps approaching 39%. The same measure before the coronavirus pandemic was usually in the range 34–35% of GDP.

Pandemic-era spending led to a spike above 40% for two years. However, true to the then–government's word, most of that spending was temporary. The huge deficits of that era did leave a legacy in the form of ongoing interest expense on the resulting public debt. But otherwise, the pandemic can't be blamed for expenditure now being about 4 percentage points of GDP higher than before it. That is a massive $100 billion plus, every year.

These increases have happened mainly at the federal level, although a good portion of the additional expenditure amounts to the federal government effectively bankrolling state expenditures and responsibilities. An examination of program expenditure points to the seeds of increased federal spending being sown long ago.

Looking back to 2012-13 we see the rapid growth of expenses on disability support (the NDIS), aged care, child care, schools, public hospitals, pharmaceutical benefits and medical benefits — all programs that have been boosted by new policy initiatives since 2012-13 to roll out new social benefits or enhance existing ones.

The welfare state has been on a roll, but in addition defence and funding of state infrastructure projects have increased rapidly, as has debt interest expense as a result of the budget deficits. All these programs together accounted for 35% of federal own-purpose expenditure in 2012-13 but for 63% of the dollar increase in annual expenditure up to 2024-25. Each item has its own story, and we wouldn't suggest that the growth was all avoidable. For example, some of it reflects population ageing and the increase in defence is a normalisation from a historically low level.

However, the growth in social spending also includes wasteful and ineffective spending. That growth reflects the priorities of an earlier Labor government, and the subsequent Coalition government largely went along with it or felt they had to. Unfortunately this political dynamic has created a situation where the main sources of growth in terms of employment and spending in the economy have been focussed in areas that are relatively low productivity (the care economy in particular).

To make matters worse, the current Labor government is doubling down on its previous spending increases in most areas. Aged care, childcare and Medicare are all areas where the government has unveiled substantial new spending commitments. The government has agreed to increase its share of Gonski school funding. And it has promised or hopes to go further with 'free' TAFE and universal child care, while pressures for further increases in defence can be expected.

Of course, this additional spending, though significant in its own right, is dwarfed by the growing costs of the NDIS. The CIS warned long ago that the NDIS was likely to grow far faster than had been predicted at the time. Despite these prescient warnings, both sides of politics have made only modest efforts to rein in the NDIS monster. Consequently, there are good reasons to be sceptical of rosy predictions of the NDIS cost–curve flattening (although staying at a level well above the growth of the economy) without substantial intervention.

It should be noted as well, despite the rapidly burgeoning costs, many participants and providers in the scheme report dissatisfaction with how the scheme is being managed. While increases in spending in individual programs and areas are the measure of the increase in the size of government, this is not the root cause. The bigger issue is the culture of dependency and entitlement has taken root in the population and political behaviour has become only too willing to accommodate and encourage it.

We have reached a point where a sizeable proportion of the voting age population — perhaps more than half — is dependent on government directly or indirectly through social benefits and employment for most of their income. It is difficult to see the current government reversing this trend without a major change of mindset. While there is some hope for the broader centre left of politics in movements like the 'abundance agenda', left wing parties across the western world have become the parties of higher taxes and bigger government.

Despite the political difficulties, the economic and social consequences of the growth in government spending and dependency on government will have to be faced one day. The economic consequences include the unrelenting pressure for more deficits and more debt, which will make the economy more vulnerable to future crises and the government less able to respond. Governments' insatiable appetite for revenue also creates more pressure for taxes to rise, which in turn saps incentives for work, saving and investment — and thereby potentially compounds the problem of weak productivity growth.

The simple fact is that people respond to incentives. When the incentives encourage innovation, investment and ingenuity, people respond by increasing productivity. Our living standards grow. However, when the incentives encourage us to fight over the distribution of the pie, even as it shrinks, the rot of entitlement and waste sinks in.

This opinion piece was originally published in 2025 by the *Canberra Times.*

Blame bigger government for falling living standards

Nicholas Moore and Tom Switzer (2025)

Across the West, incumbent governments have been falling, from New Zealand and the UK to the US — and most likely Canada later this year. While each government had its own flaws, common to all was broad public dissatisfaction with declining living standards amidst sustained inflation. Similar pressures face Australian governments. Understanding why this is happening is important. The fact is the current cost-of-living malaise in Australia is the result of years of well-intended bipartisan policies that have expanded the role of government at the cost of long-term productivity.

Many people roll their eyes at the mention of the word, but productivity matters. Simply put, productivity means output per hour worked; and without growth in productivity, our living standards deteriorate. Australia has been here before. Indeed, a combination of sluggish productivity, inflation and economic stagnation was the norm almost 50 years ago. That crisis prompted a group of thinkers, including newspapers (such as the AFR) and think tanks (such as the Centre for Independent Studies), to promote a reform agenda of deregulation, privatisation, fiscal prudence and economic liberalisation. Political leaders on both sides took note.

The result was about three decades of growth with low inflation, low unemployment and, according to the Productivity Commission, no great widening in inequality. In real terms, national income per capita from the early 1990s to the early 2010s increased by two thirds. Since then, however, Australia has experienced stagnant real wages and a productivity drought.

So what can be done? Substantial productivity improvements are still possible, but the regulation of our economy is extraordinary and its impact is colossal.

Take the housing affordability crisis. Housing is Australia's largest asset class at $11 trillion, and the average household's single largest expenditure. By way of comparison, our installed electricity system is worth a few hundred billion dollars and the energy transition may double that amount. Yet work by our researchers has shown that in our major cities, approximately half the cost of our housing (either buying or renting) comes from government taxes and regulations. In particular, planning approvals restrict supply, driving up the price.

As is often the case, the ones who suffer most from these barriers to entry are the most disadvantaged, the poor and the young. Planning approval seeks to address real issues, but the level of harm caused by restrictions on housing supply dwarfs any real or imagined benefits delivered by our current planning process. The solution to our housing problem is straightforward, though it has proven a hard nut to crack in practice. The NSW and Victorian governments are showing the way by recognising the cost to the broader public and reducing planning controls and the role of local councils — which only consider their own narrow geographic interest.

Then there is education. When the Gonski recommendations were presented to the government in 2011, hardly anyone in Canberra argued seriously against the extra billions of dollars dedicated to improving schools' outcomes. And yet, despite the hard work of our dedicated educators, the outcomes not only continue to be poor but have made, at best, no measurable improvement and, at worst, have gone backwards. According to domestic and international testing, almost 40% of our children are on track to leave school without basic skills essential for higher learning, especially in literacy and numeracy. When two out of five future workers can't read properly or do simple maths, it's no wonder productivity is declining. And it's especially tragic that children from disadvantaged backgrounds make up a disproportional number of the struggling 40%. CIS research has proven the best ways for teachers to maximise students' learning of reading, maths, and managing classrooms. This is all about focusing on the fundamentals and teaching in ways that are explicit, with high expectations, and doing away with fashionable but ineffective educational fads.

It's encouraging to see government and non-government schools beginning to abandon those fads. But the rate of change feels glacial. Housing and schools are far from the only areas of concern. A lack of action — or, indeed, the wrong actions — in key policy areas such as energy, infrastructure, industrial relations and taxation have all contributed to our productivity drought. In these areas, Australia's policy choices have made things worse.

Indeed, given the cost-of-living problems, there are increasing calls for state action that will further wind back the success of past reforms. In the US, for instance, the new administration will hurt the economy with import and immigration restrictions. More restrictions on Australian commerce, such as housing and rental controls, would also be counterproductive.

Finally, budget responsibility still matters. Deficit spending in excess of revenue at a time of record terms of trade and full employment must lead to inflation and increased debt. And with high interest rates, our heavy debt burden will seriously impinge on our government's ability to protect our people and support our disadvantaged citizens. In any event, increasing debt can only be paid for by productivity growth; so once again we come back to the same problem. Our future prosperity depends on getting productivity back on track.

Some problems in life seem impossible to solve, but our productivity problems are of our own making and our history shows that we can resolve them. The longer we wait to solve these problems, the greater the cost to all Australians, especially our young and disadvantaged.

This opinion piece was originally published in 2025 by the *Australian Financial Review.*

Gorillas In The Mist: How government obscures its spending

Gene Tunny (2024)

Executive Summary

The paper highlights the increasing trend of federal and state governments in Australia engaging in substantial 'off-budget' spending, with plans to spend over $110 billion off-budget over the next four years. This reflects a growing government desire to intervene across the economy, often through activist industrial policy.

Off-budget measures can be used to obscure the true financial position of the government, reducing transparency and accountability. Information about these activities is frequently shielded under claims of commercial-in-confidence.

These activities inherently involve risks, as they are not always for commercial reasons, which can lead to underperforming investments, write-offs, or bad debts. They also create long-term fiscal risks through contingent liabilities that are not fully appreciated. For instance, the HELP loan programme already sees about one dollar in every six lent out written off by the Federal government.

Off-budget spending contributes to higher debt and interest payments, potentially leading to higher taxes which can reduce productivity and living standards. It also may worsen inflation.

Government financing vehicles, such as the Clean Energy Finance Corporation (CEFC) and National Reconstruction Fund Corporation (NRFC), are increasingly used for policy goals like climate and industrial policy. However, this can result in inefficient use of resources and underperforming investments, representing substantial opportunity costs.

Many off-budget activities lack a clear market failure justification. Activist industrial policy measures undertaken off-budget risk the government picking losers rather than winners.

Recommendations

The paper recommends measures to improve transparency and oversight:

- Better reporting and transparency of off-budget activities.
- Quantification of fiscal risks.
- More rigorous oversight of government investments and their economic implications.

Assessment of off-budget activities

Transparency and accountability

Off-budget entities allow governments to gain distance and political cover for activities for which they should be accountable. Issues include the potential for commercial-in-confidence claims to restrict information and increased complexity in tracking financial exposure. Examples like the Northern Australia Infrastructure Facility (NAIF) and the National Broadband Network (NBN) have faced criticism for inadequate transparency and political influence. A recommendation is to develop a consistent standard for reporting concessional finance across government-owned entities.

Balance sheet risks

Off-budget activities can reduce the government's net financial worth, though this loss may not be fully reflected in the fiscal balance. Investments directed at policy objectives, not commercial ones, carry significant risks of underperforming loans or write-offs. The HELP programme is a key example, where revaluations of un-repaid loans affect the government's net financial worth, but this is not readily identifiable as a cost of HELP in budget documents. The proliferation of off-budget financing agencies adds risk to government balances. Although the federal government is required to declare risks (contingent liabilities) in the Statement of Risks, they do not always quantify the possible size of the fiscal risk.

Underlying economic consequences

Since these activities often result in losses, they ultimately lead to higher debt and net interest payments, implying higher future taxation, which causes efficiency losses. They also risk diverting economic resources away from more efficient uses, leading to lower productivity and living standards.

- The investment performance of federal off-budget entities illustrates poor returns for taxpayers. For example, by offering concessional finance, the government sacrifices between 2 to nearly 4 percentage points compared to lending at market rates, corresponding to a loss of $211–356 million in 2022–23.
- Investments are often politically motivated rather than commercially motivated. Examples include the Snowy Hydro 2.0 project, which is significantly behind schedule and over budget, and the NBN, which failed a credible cost-benefit analysis.
- While some off-budget spending, such as income-contingent loans for higher education (HECS-HELP), may be justified by addressing market failures, the rationale is deficient in many cases, as there is often no lack of financing for sound projects.
- The International Monetary Fund (IMF) has raised concerns about the proliferation of off-budget entities in the current macroeconomic climate due to transparency issues and their potential to add to fiscal stimulus, contributing to inflationary pressures.

Adverse economic consequences include:

- Lower productivity and living standards due to diversion of resources.
- An additional reduction in living standards from the taxation needed

to cover losses.

- Adverse macroeconomic impacts if extra-budgetary activity leads to an inappropriate fiscal stance, given economic conditions.

Conclusion

The recent proliferation of off-budget activities since the 2008 financial crisis is concerning, as it allows politicians to minimise the direct budget impact while accumulating significant risks on the balance sheet. This results in high opportunity costs, underperforming investments, harm to accountability and transparency, and complicates the RBA's task of controlling inflation. While not all such transactions are bad, they are being used more than is justified.

Greater disclosure on the nature, opportunity costs, and risks of off-budget activities is essential.

Specific recommendations for greater transparency include:

- Quantification of the fiscal risks associated with off-budget activities (e.g., in the federal government's Statement of Risks).
- An itemisation of the components of revaluations affecting the general government sector in budget papers.
- The identification of the public debt interest cost of budget measures.
- Further analysis by the PBO and Treasury of the implications of off-budget activities.
- Developing a consistent standard for the reporting of concessional finance across government-owned entities.

This is an edited extract of a 2024 Centre for Independent Studies research paper. The full paper can be found at https://www.cis.org.au/publication/gorillas-in-the-mist-how-government-obscures-its-spending/

Section Four: Social Spending

Robert Carling

This chapter collects several critical analyses of the Australian welfare state and social spending programs, providing an overarching perspective on their escalating costs, ineffectiveness, structural inefficiencies, and long-term unsustainability. The papers argue that, without radical, market-oriented reforms, the financial burden of the current system — including health, education, disability support, and pensions — will become fiscally unmanageable.

Some of these papers were written more than 10 years ago in the context of a CIS program aimed specifically at reducing the size of government. They remain as relevant today as they were then, as much of the subsequent growth in government has come from these programs in education, health, disability care, aged care and child care, for example. A troubling new trend in the welfare state has been the increased emphasis on universal in-kind services — exactly the model that is challenged in this chapter. The latest example is the Prime Minister's ambition for universal child care.

The core message of the studies in this chapter identifies two major problems across the spectrum of social programs. Firstly, there is an issue of misallocation and inefficiency, exemplified by the pervasive tax-welfare 'churn'. This churn, particularly in government-subsidised services like health and schooling, means middle- and high-income earners pay tax only to receive benefits back, achieving no redistribution and adding administrative complexity and cost. The proposed solution across various schemes is a shift towards tighter means-testing or self-funding models, using the resulting savings to reduce taxes or improve targeted support for those most in need.

Secondly, the chapter warns of the dynamic cost and unsustainable trajectory of current arrangements. The Age Pension's generous assets test exclusions, the exponential growth of the National Disability Insurance Scheme, and the consistently rising real expenditure on Medicare and public hospitals all point to a looming fiscal crisis. The solutions put forward are structural and systemic, advocating for market-based mechanisms such as Health Savings Accounts and private insurance vouchers for health, including the family home in the pension assets test, and implementing reforms to increase the effectiveness and efficiency of education spending.

In essence, the collection argues that maintaining the principle of fairness — ensuring equitable access to necessary care — requires the government to abandon the flawed principle of universal or quasi-universal provision that benefits those who can afford to contribute to their own services. By making tough political decisions to implement these reforms, Australia can secure a more efficient, targeted, and financially sustainable social safety net for the future.

Ending the Churn: A tax/welfare swap

John Humphreys (2009)

Executive Summary

The Australian welfare system, including health, education, and cash payments, costs over $250 billion per year. Approximately half of this spending is pointless 'churn,' where the same person pays taxes and receives benefits. The primary issue is 'services churn,' where middle- and high-income earners pay tax and receive government-subsidised health and schooling.

By eliminating middle-class welfare in exchange for income tax cuts, the government could reduce tax and welfare by roughly $80 billion without leaving anybody worse off. The costs of churn include direct economic costs (administration, compliance, and efficiency) and non-economic costs (lower self-esteem, reduced individual responsibility, political rent-seeking, and lack of transparency).

The biggest argument against churn is the dynamic cost: the current welfare system is unsustainable and will require massive tax increases, drastic service cuts, or systemic reform within 40 years. The easiest solution is to means-test government benefits, including health and school services, and offset this with an increase in the income tax-free threshold to ensure no family is financially worse off. Removing churn provides economic, non-economic, and dynamic benefits without any difficult trade-offs.

Introduction

The Australian welfare state costs more than $250 billion annually, with up to $140 billion being taken from and given back to the exact same taxpayers, a welfare 'churn' that achieves no redistribution. The greatest costs are the dynamic effects, specifically long-term unsustainability and lower-quality services. The suggested reform is a tax-welfare swap, where some individuals accept fewer government benefits in exchange for paying less tax. This can be achieved through either an 'opt-out' or a 'means-test' swap. By removing middle-class welfare churn, it would be possible to offer up to $80 billion in income tax cuts and increase the tax-free threshold to over $100,000 for some workers.

The tax-welfare churn

Australia's complex tax and welfare system, with 125 taxes and dozens of schemes, allows the anomaly of tax-welfare churn to go unnoticed. Churn occurs when the government takes tax and provides welfare to the same person with no redistribution of income.

How much churn?

Estimates suggest that about 50% to 56% of government welfare is churn. Based on 2007–08 figures, total annual churn is estimated to be between $127 billion and $142 billion. Out of the total individual income tax of $142 billion in 2007–08, about $78 billion (55%) was churned back, while only $64 billion (45%) went to redistribution or public goods. The paper posits that it should be possible to reduce churn by up to $80 billion per year.

Cash churn v services churn

- **Cash churn** occurs when people pay tax and receive cash back (e.g., family benefits), primarily due to benefits paid to middle- and high-income families. While Australia has the lowest level of cash churn in the OECD, it still accounts for about 13% of income tax ($18.4 billion) being returned as cash to the payers.
- **Services churn** occurs when people pay tax and receive money back as

subsidised services, mainly through government health and schooling. Services provision is generally not means-tested, forming the bulk of 'middle-class welfare'. Services churn is three times larger than cash churn, accounting for about 42% of income tax ($59.6 billion).

The case for reform: why churn is bad.

Churn's costs are real, and while the direct economic costs are relatively small, the dynamic effects are the most important. Services churn, unlike cash churn, reduces individual control over spending, which decreases competition and lowers the quality of services. Furthermore, the non-means-tested nature of services is unsustainable as the population ages and demand for healthcare increases.

Direct economic costs

Churn increases costs by requiring money to flow unnecessarily around the economy.

Administration and compliance costs.

The costs associated with the 'tax army' (administration and compliance) and the bureaucracy for welfare, health, education, and tax exceed **$10 billion** annually. By removing churn, people would deal with either the tax or the welfare system, but not both, which could save over $1 billion per year, even with a modest 10% cost reduction.

Economic cost of higher taxes

The tax-welfare churn adds approximately $130 billion to Australia's annual tax bill. The economic efficiency costs are low because reducing churn does not necessarily change high 'effective marginal tax rates' (EMTRs) that disincentivise work. However, where services churn forces people to get the 'wrong' service or spend too much, it distorts decision-making and creates an economic efficiency cost. Since churn has no clear benefits, any efficiency cost is too high.

Non-economic costs

These costs are considered more important than economic costs by some sociologists, though they are difficult to quantify.

Social costs of dependency

Churn increases reliance on the government, reducing personal responsibility. This has a negative effect on recipients through:

- **Lower self-esteem** and a socialisation into a mentality of dependence.
- **Worse behaviour** due to 'learned helplessness' and a high time preference, leading to a greater preference for immediate satisfaction (e.g., drug addiction).
- **Undermining social capital** by 'crowding out' voluntary civil society groups like Friendly Societies, replacing them with impersonal bureaucratic departments and contributing to social exclusion.

The solution: a tax-welfare swap

Opts-out v means test

The two strategies are the 'opt-out' swap and the 'means-test' swap. The **'means-test' swap** is the preferred method: government benefits are means-tested, and the resulting savings are used to compensate people with income tax cuts.

From theory to practice

Services churn (health and schooling) accounts for about three-quarters of all churn and is the focus for reform. Cash churn could be addressed by increasing the tax-free threshold to remove cash welfare recipients entirely from the tax system.

Health spending churn

In 2006–07, government health spending was a subsidy of nearly $3,000 per person per year. Under the reform, low-income earners would retain the full subsidy, while high-income earners would receive a tax cut to afford private health insurance or services.

School spending churn

In 2006–07, the government spent $58.2 billion on schooling. The subsidy was about $12,000 per government student and $6,300 per private student. Removing churn means low-income earners retain the full subsidy (keeping government schools free), while higher-income earners receive tax cuts to cover the true cost of schooling.

Benefits from the reform

The reform would ensure that people receiving benefits do not pay income tax, and vice versa. The tax-free threshold would be significantly increased, dependent on family situation; for example, a person with one child in government school could see their threshold rise to $76,000. This proposal offers a rare opportunity for $80 billion worth of tax cuts while guaranteeing no family is made worse off.

Conclusion

Addressing tax-welfare churn does not involve the difficult political trade-offs found in other policy areas. The $80 billion churn associated with income tax can be fixed by means-testing benefits and compensating people with offsetting income tax cuts. This approach provides lower administrative and compliance costs, greater economic efficiency, fewer social and political costs, greater transparency, and a more sustainable, efficient, and effective health and schooling system.

This is an edited extract of a 2009 Centre for Independent Studies research paper. The full paper can be found at https://www.cis.org.au/publication/ending-the-churn-a-taxwelfare-swap/

The Age-Old Problem of Old Age: Fixing the Pension

Simon Cowan and Matthew Taylor (2015)

The Age Pension is the largest single payment made by the federal government, with annual expenditure predicted to rise to nearly $50 billion by 2017–18. Age Pension expenditure is large, growing, not sufficiently targeted — meaning those in need are not helped as much as they could be — and is not sustainable. The real cost has increased by 35% between 2007–08 and 2014–15 because at least 70% of people of retirement age receive some form of pension.

The current system creates inequity because the exemption of the family home from the pension assets means test means homeowners have substantially higher net worth — often nine times that of non-homeowners — but often receive similar pension entitlements. The perverse incentives mean the vast majority of pensioners do not utilise their home equity to support their retirement.

A three-point strategy is proposed to remove these distortions and improve living standards:

1. Include the family home in the assets test and abolish the homeowner/non-homeowner distinction.
2. Help pensioners access reverse mortgages by legislating for a default product (guaranteed or insured by government).
3. Include the reverse mortgage payment in the income test by deeming income from the default product.

The modelling of these reforms indicates a Taxpayer Saving of $14.5 billion (reducing annual expenditure from $42.2 billion to $27.7 billion). Furthermore, nearly 98% of pensioners (2,371,000) would gain an average of $5,924 annually, allowing the government to raise the pension base rate for those most in need.

What is the pension for?

The belief that the pension is a 'right' is mistaken; pensions are paid by current taxpayers, and the welfare system's fundamental principle is that help should be prioritised for those who cannot help themselves. The pension should function as a safety net for people with limited wealth, be tightly means-tested, and focus on alleviating poverty. In practice, it operates as a quasi-universal scheme that boosts retirement incomes for many older Australians with substantial assets.

Approximately 10% of people in Australia are on the Age Pension, with the number of recipients growing by more than 55% between 1993 and 2013. Some estimates suggest that 70% to 80% of people of retirement age receive some form of the pension. Just under 60% of Age Pensioners are on the full rate, and nearly all of those who are assets-tested off the full rate are homeowners (97%).

The adequacy of the pension is a central policy consideration, but policy must also address undesirable incentives and minimise unnecessary burdens on taxpayers. The base level of the single pension is in line with common measures of adequacy, and the data does not make a strong case for an increase in the full rate based on the poverty of pensioners.

The data shows that income test thresholds are too generous for those with substantial incomes. It is difficult to justify providing support to people with incomes at nearly twice the poverty line if the main purpose of the pension is to ensure no pensioner lives in poverty.

The total real cost of the Age Pension has increased by 35% between 2007–08 and 2014–15. Cost pressures will increase dramatically as the ratio of working age people to every person over 65 falls from 4.5 to just 2.7 by

2055. The maturation of the superannuation system will not substantially reduce these fiscal pressures, with one estimate suggesting it will reduce total pension spending by only 6%. Furthermore, the political impact of an ageing population is likely to exacerbate the trend of politicians promising pension increases, which are not included in future cost estimates.

Homeownership among retirees

More than 80% of retirees own their own home, and over 75% of pensioners are homeowners. The total value of pensioner home equity is roughly $625 billion, and the home dominates asset holdings for many pensioners, representing over 70% of their wealth. The current system treats people with $500,000 or $600,000 in assets as being in the same position as those with less than $10,000.

The principal residence exclusion from the assets test

The exclusion of the principal residence from the assets test should be fixed for two reasons: fairness and the potential to greatly improve the living standards of pensioners. For full-rate pensioners, homeowners have more than nine times the net worth of non-homeowners, yet they receive similar pension payments. Including the home in the assets test would move over 40% of full-rate pensioners to the part-rate and many others off the pension altogether. Excluding the home also creates artificial distinctions between asset classes, encourages over-investment in housing equity, and is a driving factor behind Australia's housing affordability problem.

The family home is an untapped asset

The family home is not widely viewed as a retirement savings tool, with only 11% of Australians planning to sell it and only 8% planning to draw down equity via a reverse mortgage to fund retirement. Most older Australians prefer to 'age in place'. A key motivation for not utilising home equity is the desire to pass the home onto their children (a bequest motive), but the government cannot afford to subsidise bequests by providing pensions to people who have assets to support themselves.

Reverse mortgages

There is enormous unused capacity to utilise home equity, as less than 1.1% of people of retirement age have taken out a reverse mortgage. Given the tens of billions the government pays in pensions, there is a strong financial incentive to support alternative income sources. The government should regulate and incentivise a standard default reverse mortgage annuity product, provided by banks or superannuation funds but guaranteed or insured by government, to ensure pensioners are never forced to sell their home. The scheme must be combined with deeming income from the reverse mortgage in the income test, which accepts that not all houses of similar value have the same income-producing capabilities.

This is an edited extract of a 2015 Centre for Independent Studies research paper. The full paper can be found at https://www.cis.org.au/publication/the-age-old-problem-of-old-age-fixing-the-pension-2/

The New Leviathan: A National Disability Insurance Scheme

Andrew Baker (2012)

Executive Summary

The National Disability Insurance Scheme (NDIS) intended to provide no-fault insurance cover for Australians with a severe or profound disability. While a worthwhile endeavour with broad support, at the time this paper was written, the scheme had not received the scrutiny such a large and expensive undertaking deserves. This report predicted that the NDIS would be a 'monster' government programme, growing to become the 'new leviathan' of the Australian welfare state.

- Official cost estimates have been consistently revised upwards, with the Productivity Commission (PC) ultimately estimating a gross annual cost of $15 billion for 411,000 people.
- These figures are misleading as they were based on 2009–10 data and did not account for wage increases, price inflation, or population growth up to the full operational date of 2018–19.
- A review by the Australian Government Actuary (AGA) estimated the 2018–19 cost at $22 billion (gross) for 441,000 people.
- However, this figure still likely underestimated the true cost as it excluded financial risks, notably the ageing population and 'back-end growth' (NDIS recipients choosing to remain on the scheme rather than moving to aged care).
- Political pressure from over a million people who will initially miss out (e.g., those on the Disability Support Pension or aged over 65) also threatens to expand the scheme's eligibility and supports, driving up costs.

- Based on case studies of similar schemes, NDIS expenditure is likely to grow at least around 6% per year. The report estimates the scheme will cost approximately $29.5 billion per year by 2023–24, providing supports to around 500,000 people, including the administrative costs for over 8,000 bureaucrats.
- The report calls for reforms to minimise expenses and identify offsets to manage the scheme's rapid real growth.

Introduction

In 2009, Australian governments spent approximately $7 billion on disability care and support, with an additional $15.5 billion on income support. Despite this extraordinary spending, there remains a substantial lack of support and services. The PC found the current system to be underfunded, unfair, fragmented, and inefficient, leading to 'Soviet-style rationing' of services. The system is characterised by paternalistic policies and excessive red tape, giving people with disability little control over their supports. The PC argued that the substantial costs of lifetime care necessitate pooling the risks and costs to alleviate the current crisis, as the cost of doing nothing would increase future liabilities for all governments.

The case for the NDIS was established following the 2008 Australia 2020 Summit. Reports highlighted poor outcomes for people with disability in areas like education and employment. The Disability Investment Group (DIG) found the sector faced a 'death spiral' due to increasing demand and an ageing population. The DIG recommended a new social insurance approach, which led to the PC's feasibility study and subsequent report. The PC called for a systemic overhaul, projecting that the NDIS would have net economic benefits through efficiency gains like reduced 'bed blocking' in hospitals and increased economic participation.

Scope of the NDIS

The NDIS was intended to provide no-fault insurance cover and lifetime care and support for Australian residents under the pension age with a severe or profound disability, based on assessed need.

- The PC estimated around 411,000 people would receive funded supports based on 2009–10 figures.
- The NDIS will fund supports that meet additional disability-related needs to help people engage in the community.
- Supports more appropriately met by other systems—such as health, hospital care, education, public transport, and the Disability Support Pension (DSP)—will be excluded from the scheme.

The word 'insurance' in the scheme's name is a misnomer. While based on insurance principles (pooling resources for low-frequency, high-cost events), it is better understood as a social security or entitlement scheme with strict eligibility definitions. The PC's blueprint departs from traditional insurance by recommending 'no general requirement for a front-end deductible' or co-payments, which would typically help control costs.

The cost

The PC's cost estimates were based on constant 2009–10 dollars. This creates a disconnect with the full implementation of the scheme, as the estimates do not account for general wage growth, price inflation, or population increases by the full operational date of 2018–19, and subsequent years. Consequently, the widely used figures underestimate the scheme's true budgetary cost by billions of dollars and the eligible population by tens of thousands.

Initial cost estimates have been consistently revised upwards.

- The DIG (2009) estimated a gross cost of $10.8 billion.
- The PC's final report estimated the gross cost at $13.5 billion, which increased to $15 billion after accounting for the Community Sector Wage Case (SaCS) increase.

The AGA's revised gross cost estimate for the NDIS in 2018–19 was $22 billion for 441,000 people. This figure is significant, making the NDIS potentially a larger programme than Medicare in budgetary terms for 2009–10. Accounting for annual growth of 6% (based on other schemes), the NDIS could cost around $30 billion by 2023–24. (Although Baker was ahead of everyone else, even he did not see the full dimensions of the cost explosion that was coming, because the projected cost of NDIS in 2024-5 is $49 billion and is still climbing steeply — Ed.)

Wage increases, price inflation and population growth

Since disability support is highly labour-intensive, wage increases are a major cost driver. Indexing the PC's $15 billion 2009–10 gross cost to 2018–19 using average wage and price growth adds an estimated $7 billion, raising the cost to roughly $22 billion and aligning with the AGA's estimate.

The PC's eligible population estimate of 411,000 (based on 2009–10) would increase by an additional 30,000 people when factoring in general population growth to 2018–19.

After adjusting for wage increases, price inflation, and population growth, the NDIS's projected cost in 2018–19 is estimated to be approximately $22.5 billion.

The PC recommended that people over the pension age be covered by the aged care system. However, the AGA warned of a risk of 'back-end growth' where NDIS participants choose to remain on the scheme for the better supports, which would add thousands of people and hundreds of millions of dollars by 2018–19.

Politics and populism

The differential treatment for people with disability above and below the pension age is a continuing source of concern and political pressure. The total eligible population is estimated at 451,000 people, which leaves over one million voters (500,000 DSP recipients and 600,000 over-65s with a severe disability) who will miss out, creating a vested interest in seeing a more generous NDIS.

The NDIS's scope is tightly defined to meet 'reasonable and necessary specialist disability support needs,' excluding services met by other systems. The AGA noted a significant risk from high public expectations that may not align with the 'reasonable and necessary' emphasis, potentially driving up costs.

The continual expansion of funded supports beyond original intent is called 'mission creep' or 'scope creep'. For instance, including funding for integration aides in schools would increase the cost of the scheme by over $400 million every year.

The PC recommended an internal merits review process to ensure long-term sustainability and prevent decisions that unreasonably impose costs on the scheme. However, this internal approach was criticised, with calls for a totally independent tribunal to review decisions on their merits. The PC was concerned that an external mechanism could undermine the financial integrity of the NDIS by expanding the scheme's scope.

Case studies

Medicare Australia

Medicare expenditure grew at an average of 7.5% per year between 1983 and 2008, well above inflation, driven by increased utilisation and price rises. This growth serves as a warning of the difficulty the government may face in controlling NDIS costs.

New Zealand's Accident Compensation Corporation

New Zealand's no-fault insurance scheme (ACC) saw its outstanding claims liability grow from $6 billion to $17.5 billion between 1999–00 and 2009–10. Total expenditure grew at an average annual rate of 10.5% over this period, driven by claims exceeding expectations and above-inflation increases in healthcare costs.

Victoria's Transport Accident Commission

Even a more restricted scheme like Victoria's TAC experienced significant expenditure growth, with benefits increasing at an average annual rate of 5.8% between 1998–99 and 2010–11.

Private health insurance increases.

The costs of private health insurance have also risen at an average rate of 6.1% per year between 2001 and 2012, indicating a high rate of increase in health-related costs.

The cost of the NDIS: 2018–19 and beyond

Assuming a conservative real expenditure growth rate of 6% on top of the AGA's 2018–19 cost estimate, the NDIS cost would reach approximately $29.5 billion by 2023–24. The paper concludes the NDIS will be a $30 billion scheme within a decade of its inception.

Taming leviathan

To manage the rapid cost growth, it is crucial to:

- Prevent scope creep by maintaining the scheme's boundaries in age restrictions, disability severity, and funded supports, which requires political will.
- Address the high cost of labour by reducing supply barriers, potentially through establishing a live-in caregiver programme or reforming working holiday visas.
- Consider implementing a limited co-payment or excess for initial assessment claims (refundable if successful) to minimise start-up costs and reduce unnecessary demand.
- Generate administrative savings by integrating back-office functions of the NDIA with the Commonwealth Department of Human Services (DHS), following the example of the Medicare/Centrelink merger.
- Reform the DSP to align its objectives and incentives with the NDIS's goal of returning people to the workforce.

Conclusion

The NDIS has not received the necessary scrutiny. Post-implementation, expenditure is highly likely to grow at around 6% each year. Given the scheme's sheer size, every effort must be made to maximise its economic benefits while minimising cost drivers and identifying offsets.

This is an edited extract of a 2012 Centre for Independent Studies research paper. The full paper can be found at https://www.cis.org.au/publication/the-new-leviathan-a-national-disability-insurance-scheme-3/

Saving Medicare but NOT as we know it

Dr Jeremy Sammut (2013)

Executive Summary

Real combined federal, state, and territory government spending on health (adjusted for inflation) increased by 80% from $53 billion in 2000–01 to more than $90 billion in 2010–11. Although public health expenditure was contained during the economic 'long boom' (rising from 5.6% to 6.4% of GDP) , a new era of lower growth will make paying for continued increases more difficult. Private health reforms have not fundamentally shifted the balance, with government funding increasing by 0.8% of GDP, outstripping the 0.2% increase in non-government funding.

The Intergenerational Reports show that rising health costs will unsustainably increase the size of government. To address this, the paper recommends cutting Medicare down to size by:

- Boosting the efficiency of public health services.
- Better targeting of public health spending.
- Expanding the role played by private health care financing.

Specific reforms include: downsizing the federal Department of Health; privatising select public hospital facilities ; reintroducing Medicare co-payments for GP consultations ; and imposing a means test on Medicare entitlements.

For a 'big bang' reform, the paper proposes a New Medicare that reconfigures spending into two streams for younger Australians: Health Savings Accounts (HSAs) and high-deductible private health insurance vouchers. This would transform the existing scheme into an age-limited and targeted programme for current retirees and near-retirees.

Introduction: The cost curve

- Real national health expenditure increased by 68% between 2000–01 and 2010–11, growing 70% faster than real average GDP, and consuming 9.3% of GDP.
- Over two-thirds (69.1%) of total national health spending is through government programmes.
- Nearly 70% of the public health spend ($62 billion in 2010–11) funded public hospital care, the Medical Benefits Scheme (MBS), and the Pharmaceutical Benefits Scheme (PBS).
- Long public hospital waiting times are a structural feature of Medicare, caused by inefficiencies that allow unrestricted access to GP services for minor health needs. Access to 'free' hospital care is rationed by queues to control the total cost.
- Both the public and private systems 'over-provide' for the minor health needs of the majority while 'under-providing' protection against serious illness for the minority of patients with major health needs.

The ageing challenge

- The unprecedented impact of the ageing population is the subject of the Intergenerational Reports (IGRs).
- The IGRs model the long-term effects of rising health spending on federal budget sustainability, defining sustainability as the ability to fund existing government programmes out of existing revenue at current tax rates.

High and inefficient spending

- The Commonwealth tightly caps funding for state public hospital care to offset the large and escalating cost of its own open-ended programmes, the MBS and PBS.
- No federal government has maintained a 50% share of public hospital operating costs as Medicare's designers intended.
- The public hospital system operates with a productivity gap of 20% to 25% between the least and most efficient facilities.

Averting the fiscal crisis in health

- Governments will struggle to pay for the rising quantity of increasingly sophisticated health care due to the ageing population and medical innovation.
- The stress on budgets will lead to stricter funding restrictions and more extensive rationing of services.
- The appropriate response is a dual-pronged reform: (1) shifting responsibility for health costs off government budgets, and (2) incorporating design features that boost efficiency.
- A financially sustainable way to fund health care is to pre-fund it over the long term by enabling people to save up and pay for it using self-financing and third-party insurance arrangements.

The 'fair go' case for reform

- The paper argues that Medicare is a theoretical entitlement to 'free and universal' access that, in reality, falls short of its promise.
- The core principle of public health subsidies for equity, ensuring no person goes without necessary care due to lack of income, should be maintained.
- Market-based health reform is necessary to increase equity, as the access problems for low-income Australians will worsen as the impact of population ageing hits.

Market-based solutions

- Market-based health reform treats health primarily as an economic problem involving the efficient use of scarce resources.
- It is not unfair to expect people to take greater responsibility for their care, as the New Medicare will provide the opportunity to accumulate the necessary resources.

Saving for sustainability

- The government-funded share of total health spending per person was

70% in 2010–11, but these funds are not being used optimally.

- Individuals must assume greater personal responsibility for managing their health spending.
- Sustainability can be improved by shifting the delivery of health care subsidies to a Health Savings Account (HSA) and a high deductible insurance voucher system.

The New Medicare

- This 'big bang' reform would split existing Medicare spending into two streams of 'New Medicare' funding:
    1. Health Savings Accounts (HSAs): Personalised, compulsory savings accounts (modelled on superannuation) with government deposits, to be used for minor health expenses.
    2. High-deductible private health insurance vouchers: Government-funded vouchers for all citizens to purchase high-deductible insurance for major costs (e.g., catastrophic illness).
- High-deductibles significantly reduce administration costs and premiums. The HSA would cover costs until the deductible is met.
- The goal is greater financial sustainability, enhanced efficiency, and improved equity.

Ten tips to TARGET30

Practical structural and programmatic reforms include:

- Downsizing the bloated Department of Health and Ageing.
- Devolving managerial and financial accountability for public hospitals from state health departments to Local Hospital Districts (LHDs).
- Privatising select public hospital facilities to create a competitive public hospital sector.
- Restricting the number of private patients treated in public hospitals to prevent 'double dipping'.
- Reintroducing in-hospital nurse training and permitting universities to offer specialist training.

- De-funding taxpayer-funded public health advocacy organisations (e.g., the National Preventive Health Agency).
- Scrapping the wasteful MBS GP management plan rebates and the Better Access to Mental Health Care programme.
- Reintroducing compulsory co-payments (inflation-adjusted to $4.26) for MBS services to curb overuse.
- Imposing a means test on Medicare entitlements.

Demand-side and supply-side

- The New Medicare would establish significant non-government funding sources and limit government exposure to rising expenditure.
- The plan is based on the idea that people will behave more prudently when they have to spend their own money on health care.

Double paying

- The shift to a savings-based system faces the obstacle of 'double paying' for younger generations, who must pay taxes for the elderly's care while saving and self-funding for their own future costs.
- Transition arrangements are needed, such as transforming the old Medicare into an age-limited targeted scheme to exclusively cover retirees or near-retirees, which could be abolished when the self-funded system matures.

Conclusion

- To avoid a fiscal crisis similar to those confronting European welfare states, Australia must act now to get people saving to pay for more of their own health care.
- The New Medicare will preserve and enhance the principle of fairness—equitable access to high-quality and affordable health services for all Australians—while reducing the unsustainable financial burden.

This is an edited extract of a 2013 Centre for Independent Studies research paper. The full paper can be found at https://www.cis.org.au/publication/saving-medicare-but-not-as-we-know-it/

Section Five: Tax Reform

Robert Carling

The analysis meticulously outlines the significant economic costs of taxation, arguing that the high marginal cost of raising tax revenue — higher for some taxes than for others — creates substantial deadweight losses and discourages productive economic activity, ultimately making the nation poorer. A major focus is placed on the structural weaknesses within the tax and welfare system, specifically highlighting the detrimental effect of high effective marginal tax rates. This problem arises from the rapid withdrawal of means-tested welfare payments as income rises, creating a powerful disincentive for Australians, particularly those on lower incomes, to work more or seek employment.

Particular attention is paid to personal income tax, which one paper characterises as a 'monster' that needs to be tamed. CIS has long been an advocate of lower and flatter marginal rates, and as reflected in this chapter while some progress has been seen in that direction there is much further to go. Another focus of the papers is personal income tax bracket creep and the case for automatic annual indexation of bracket thresholds. A cautionary note is struck against the notion that the personal income tax system is full of 'rorts' and loopholes that should be shut down. Another paper argues that while there is some scope for broadening the tax base in this way, many of the existing array of income tax concessions have a sound rationale.

The chapter champions structural reform over tax hikes, advancing a comprehensive agenda. This includes substantially raising the tax-free income threshold, lowering marginal rates and indexing thresholds, reforming complex family payments to alleviate the 'tax-welfare squeeze,' and addressing the uncompetitive nature of the company tax rate. Recognising that the cost to revenue would be large, the chapter argues that such reform would need to be phased in over time and matched by much slower growth in government spending.

Furthermore, the discussion extends to issues of fiscal federalism, where the current system of distributing Goods and Services Tax revenue among the states is scrutinised for creating complexity, perverse incentives, and friction between state and federal governments. The overall conclusion is that a principled, efficiency-driven reform of the existing tax architecture is the only path to achieving sustainable budgets and long-term prosperity.

The Case Against Tax Increases in Australia: The Growing Burden

Michael Potter (2016)

The tax burden imposed by the Commonwealth Government alone, and by all Australian governments, is above its historical levels and forecast to go well above these averages. In the past when the budget was close to balance, the tax burden was slightly lower and spending was much lower. When the tax burden rose above average, governments took significant decisions to alleviate the burden, not stand by and allow it to increase.

The budget deficit

The large budget deficit is imposing substantial costs on future taxpayers. An alternative measure of the tax burden includes the deficit, which is a form of deferred taxation, as well as the current tax burden. On this measure, the burden is well above its historical average. Tax increases to reduce the budget deficit are problematic because they just shift the tax burden from future taxpayers to current taxpayers. Instead, the historical evidence indicates that deficit reduction should occur through restricting growth in government spending:

- Spending is currently well above its historical average of 24.9%.
- During previous periods when the budget was close to balance, the federal tax burden was at or around current levels, and much lower than forecast tax levels. In those years, spending was much lower.
- In previous years when economic growth was around current levels, and unemployment around current levels, the federal tax burden was lower. In

those years, spending was also lower.

- Examining the combined tax burden of all Australian governments produces similar, or even stronger results.

Historical times of high tax burden

In the past 40 years, the federal tax burden was substantially above the average for only two periods: 2000 to 2007 and 1986 to 1988. In both of these periods, the government provided substantial tax cuts. In contrast, today the tax burden is heading well above average, and government policy decisions to date have done almost nothing to offset this tax increase. Cuts to some taxes have been largely offset by other tax increases, and proposed company tax cuts will have little effect on this upward march in the tax burden.

Historical tax reforms

Any explicit tax hikes will be in stark contrast to successful tax reforms, which have not increased the tax burden. Recent major policies to increase the tax burden have been abandoned or repealed, including the mining tax, the carbon tax, proposals to increase the GST, and (older) proposals to impose CGT on assets bought before 1985.

Historical tax cuts – were they excessive?

Historical tax cuts did not cause the current deficit or a revenue shortfall, because tax levels today are above their historical levels, despite the previous tax cuts. Tax cuts during the mining boom prevented the all-time high in the tax burden, reached in 2004–05, from being even higher. A higher tax burden might have just encouraged an increase in the size of government, with no improvement in the budget.

Should taxes be higher because of tax avoidance?

Some commentators have argued that tax avoidance nullifies the case for tax cuts. However, it is perverse to argue that the total tax burden should continue to increase because of tax avoidance. Higher taxes impose the greatest cost on people and businesses that don't avoid tax, and have no impact whatsoever on the most successful tax avoiders who pay no tax at all. There is no justification for taxes to be higher on businesses paying the full rate of tax because other unrelated companies are avoiding tax. In addition, higher tax levels are likely to exacerbate tax avoidance.

Does the state of the economy, or revenue writedowns, mean taxes should be higher?

The current budget situation is almost entirely due to government policy, not the state of the economy, as shown in official estimates of the structural budget balance. The recovery from the GFC and the end of the mining boom are having only a tiny impact on the budget. This implies that both spending and revenue levels are largely due to government decisions. High spending levels can't be blamed on the economy, and tax revenue is not weak because of the end of the mining boom, despite so-called revenue writedowns.

Removing the impact of the state of the economy, tax is likely to be at or above its long run level, while spending would be well above the historical average. Again, this does not support the case for tax increases, let alone any additional tax hikes. Taxes should not increase because of revenue writedowns, as these revisions largely reflect forecasting errors. Actual tax levels are more important than whether they were forecast correctly.

Australia is not a low taxing country

Contrary to the view of some commentators, Australia's overall tax levels are above the developed world average according to data from both the World Bank and the IMF. Data from the OECD does indicate that Australia's tax burden is below the developed world average. This is because the OECD counts social security contributions as taxes while the IMF and World Bank do not. There are good reasons to exclude these contributions from tax comparisons as they don't fully act like taxes.

Australia's revenue from personal and company tax are both well above the developed world average. These are the most inefficient taxes levied by the federal government. Regardless, developed country comparisons are flawed: they include many poorly performing economies we should not be emulating, and exclude many of our trading partners or countries in our region. Comparisons with the globe show Australia's tax levels are even less competitive.

Should Australia's tax burden increase regardless?

Despite the arguments above, should taxes nevertheless increase? The costs of taking this approach would be particularly large. Studies show higher taxes lead to reduced wages employment, innovation, investment and economic growth, while encouraging tax avoidance. Hence, based on detailed historical analysis, international comparisons, and economic studies, there are strong arguments against the tax increases set to be imposed in coming years, let alone additional tax hikes.

This is a summary of a 2016 Centre for Independent Studies research paper. The full paper can be found at https://www.cis.org.au/publication/the-case-against-tax-increases-in-australia-the-growing-burden-copy/

Why it's a Myth that Australia is a Low-taxing Country

Robert Carling (2023)

Taxation statistics released by the Australian Bureau of Statistics have been quite startling in a way that weakens the case for governments to hunt for more revenue in forthcoming federal and state budgets. The ABS reported that tax revenue shot up by 15 per cent in 2021/22, lifting revenue to almost 30 per cent of GDP, the highest since 2007/08. This refers to tax revenue at all levels of government — Commonwealth, state and local. How this national total is divided up among them is a separate issue, but ultimately it all comes from the same pockets — yours and mine.

It is of interest, however, that Commonwealth tax revenue reached 23.9 per cent of GDP, which was the cap imposed by the previous government on tax receipts and abandoned by the current government. (Receipts refer to cash and revenue to accruals, but where revenue goes, receipts will presumably follow.) The tax revenue share of GDP — whether for the Commonwealth or the national total — has been higher in the past but only six times during the resources and housing-led boom of the 2000s. Even then, the total never exceeded 30.4 per cent of GDP.

The Commonwealth budget outcomes for the first nine months of 2022/23 suggest the revenue share will rise again to something above 24.0 percent. And the only thing that might stop a new record being set for the national tax revenue ratio will be weakness in states' property stamp duty revenue. Everything else is booming. The above figures do not include record state mining royalty revenue, which arcane government finance statistics rules classify as non-tax revenue.

What all this means, quite simply, is that government coffers are brimming with revenue at a time when some economists and think tanks say taxes need to be increased — or tax cuts cancelled — to satisfy the pressure of rising government spending. To be fair, some of those people are talking as much about the future as the present, and some of the current strength of revenue is cyclical rather than structural.

However, the calls for more revenue at a time of near-record revenue strain credulity and sidestep the alternative conclusion that the number one problem is not too little revenue but too much spending. The argument so often heard is that if only taxes could be lifted by a few tens of billions of dollars a year over time, revenue would grow faster than expenditure and neatly close the gap between them, leading to balanced budgets or surpluses.

But this is something that is only ever likely to happen on an economic planner's spreadsheet. In the messy real world of budgets, such a vision is a mirage. The reality is that rising revenue would relieve the pressure to restrain expenditure. Revenue would be chasing spending and never catch up.

But isn't Australia a comparatively 'low tax' country — a claim repeated most recently in a Grattan Institute pre-budget report? There are two problems with this story. One is that it depends entirely on the many high taxing countries of Europe. Most North American and Asian countries have tax burdens below or similar to Australia's while Europe's — with the exceptions of Switzerland and Ireland — are much higher.

If we are looking for models of economic progress, would we look to Europe — and in particular, to high-taxing countries like Italy and France rather than to the low-taxing star economic performers like Switzerland and Ireland?

The claim that Australia is a low taxing country also depends heavily on the high compulsory social contributions of most other developed countries. On this test the score is: OECD average nine percentage points, Australia zero. If social contributions are taken out of the calculations, following IMF practice for international comparability, then Australia once again is not a comparatively low-taxing country.

Social contributions are mainly employee and employer contributions to state pension schemes. They are legitimately classed as a tax, but the Australian equivalent compulsory superannuation contributions — are not a tax because they constitute private funding of private retirement benefits. They do, however, have tax-like characteristics insofar as they are a compulsory deduction from take-home pay.

Compulsory super contributions are above 4 per cent of GDP and heading for more than 5 per cent as the Super Guarantee Charge rises to 12.5 per cent. If social contributions are included in comparator countries, then the SGC should be added to the Australian tax burden for comparability, and then once again we do not look like a low taxing country. Certainly, Australia's private retirement income arrangements should not be taken as an excuse to lift the tax burden to match other countries with predominantly public retirement income schemes.

Whichever way one looks at it, the proposition that Australia is a low tax country is devoid of content as a guide to policy.

This opinion piece was originally published in 2023 by the *Australian Financial Review.*

How high taxation makes us poorer

Alex Robson (2006)

Taxes tend to discourage mutually beneficial exchanges by driving a wedge between the prices suppliers wish to receive and the prices consumers are willing to pay. In free markets, voluntary exchanges are mutually beneficial and are at the heart of economic wealth creation and higher living standards. For instance, income taxes drive a wedge between the wage workers accept to supply labour and the wage employers are willing to pay them. As a result of these wedges, potential gains from mutually beneficial exchanges are left unexploited, and economic resources are diverted from higher-valued to lower-valued economic uses.

Economists refer to these unexploited gains from trade as the deadweight loss created by taxes, confirming the observation that the power to tax involves the power to destroy. While taxation is often framed as the 'price we pay for civilized society', the economic costs of raising funds — the price — must not be trivialised or conflated with the alleged benefits of government spending. A proper assessment of costs must precede the evaluation of benefits to justify any particular government programme.

A Taxonomy of Costs

Adam Smith's first principle of taxation, detailed in *The Wealth of Nations*, was that every tax ought to be contrived to take out and keep out of the pockets of the people as little as possible over and above what it brings into the public treasury. Smith recognised that even a simple tax system could have economic costs by obstructing industry and diminishing the funds that enable people to pay.

In addition to these pure economic or deadweight costs (the disincentive effects), Smith noted three other forms of taxation costs:

- Administrative and enforcement costs: The salaries and perquisites of the numerous officers required to levy a tax, which may "eat up the greater part of the produce of the tax".
- Evasion costs: The ruinous penalties incurred by individuals who unsuccessfully try to evade tax, particularly when an injudicious tax creates a strong temptation for smuggling.
- Compliance costs: The "unnecessary trouble, vexation, and oppression" that people are exposed to, which is an expense equivalent to what they would be willing to pay to redeem themselves from it.

Today, the primary reason for increased administrative and compliance costs is the growing legal and economic complexity of the tax system. The responsibility for administration has often been transferred to the private sector; for example, employers who withhold income taxes are, in effect, collecting taxes on the government's behalf. This complexity drives a growth in the number of accountants and tax specialists, many of whom are employed to prevent the government from acquiring their clients' wealth, rather than creating new wealth. Using one methodology, the Australian 'tax army' of lawyers, accountants, and tax officers was calculated to be more than three times the size of the permanent Australian Army forces.

A final category of cost is revenue-seeking or rent-seeking costs, first identified by Gordon Tullock. Since taxes redistribute wealth, various groups lobby the government either for lower taxes or for higher taxes to finance spending that may be directed their way. This activity, which is directed at redistributing, not creating, wealth, represents an additional social cost beyond the deadweight losses.

The deadweight costs of personal income tax

The deadweight cost is measured by observing that a tax on economic activity alters individual incentives. Higher income taxes reduce workers' after-tax wages. This reduction, in turn, makes other economic activities more attractive, causing workers to substitute away from work and into activities such as leisure, reduced work intensity, or do-it-yourself work. This substitution effect explains how resources are driven from higher-valued to lower-valued uses.

The deadweight loss (or excess burden) occurs when the loss in worker well-being is greater than the revenue raised by the tax. Focusing narrowly on average labour force participation rates or average hours worked can be misleading, as individuals adjust their effective labour supply in many other ways, especially in rigid industrial relations systems.

A more accurate measure of disincentive effects is the responsiveness of taxable income to changes in wages. The key parameter is the elasticity of taxable income (ETI), which measures the percentage change in taxable income when marginal tax rates change by one per cent. Studies show that taxable income is quite sensitive to changes in after-tax wages. Notably, the responsiveness tends to be higher for higher income earners (up to 0.57 for those earning over $100,000), indicating a very large economic cost per dollar of revenue raised from the most productive individuals.

Measuring the costs of taxation

The pure economic costs are quantified using two key metrics. The Average Cost of Funds (ACF) calculates the total deadweight loss as a proportion of total revenue collected. US studies of all forms of taxation estimate the ACF is between 18% and 24% of total government revenue, meaning each dollar collected costs the private sector between $1.18 and $1.24. Applying these figures to Australia's 2003–04 revenue suggests a total excess burden of taxation of at least $46 billion to $61 billion. For personal income tax alone, the estimated ACF ranges from 18% to 37%.

The Marginal Cost of Funds (MCF) is the incremental cost of raising the last dollar of tax, normalised by the incremental change in revenue. The MCF is a crucial benchmark for evaluating public projects. Any project that does not provide a percentage return higher than the MCF should not proceed, as it costs more wealth than it creates. Note that Australian governments currently do not provide official published estimates of the MCF or total deadweight costs.

Estimates of the MCF for personal income taxation

Older estimates for the MCF of personal income taxes for OECD countries were generally in the 1.2 to 1.3 range. For Australia, estimates ranged from 1.19 to 1.65. These suggest that the last dollar of government spending would need to create an economic return of at least 19% to 65% to be economically justified.

However, these traditional estimates may be too small because they can overlook how taxpayers shift compensation into non-pecuniary forms to reduce tax liability when rates rise. Taking these behavioural responses into account, one study by Feldstein on the US 1986 Tax Reform Act found the MCF for personal income taxes may be larger than 2. This implies that the last dollar of revenue raised cost the private sector more than two dollars, and that the economic return from the last dollar of government spending should exceed 200%. The MCF provides the minimal benchmark against which all public projects should be measured.

Income Taxation and Economic Growth

The costs of high personal income taxation are also evident in broader economic growth figures. Historically, no economy has achieved sustained per-capita GDP growth of 4% or more once general government spending exceeds 40% of national product. This is because the distortionary effects of high taxation overwhelm the productive benefits of the spending.

High income taxes also discourage investment in human capital (skills, productivity), which is a key driver of long-run growth. International data from the Fraser Institute strongly supports a negative correlation between tax burden and growth. OECD countries that significantly cut their taxes between 1980 and 2000 had an average per capita growth rate of over 3%, compared to only 1.7% for those that cut taxes mildly or increased them. This shows that lower marginal income tax rates are associated with higher per capita economic growth.

Conclusion

High personal income taxes create significant disincentives, ensuring that a dollar increase in government revenue ends up costing the economy far more in real terms than the dollar actually paid in taxes. The pure economic effects of a tax on the incentives to produce, work, save, invest, or consume are measured by the MCF. There is little evidence that higher taxation increases GDP growth rates, and much evidence to suggest the opposite. Finally, subsidies have a similar wealth-destroying effect to taxes, and their costs must be added to the costs of taxation for a full estimate of the cost of government intervention.

This is a summary of a 2006 Centre for Independent Studies research paper. The full paper can be found at https://www.cis.org.au/publication/taxploitation-the-case-for-income-tax-reform/

Tax Reform To Make Work Pay

Peter Saunders and Barry Maley (2004)

Executive Summary

A comprehensive reform of the Australian tax and welfare system is needed, as the current structure creates a tax-welfare squeeze that heavily penalises low- and middle-income earners for increasing their work effort. This is primarily caused by the combination of income tax and the rapid withdrawal of means-tested benefits, resulting in extremely high Effective Marginal Tax Rates (EMTRs), sometimes exceeding 60% or 70%. These disincentives are strongest for those attempting to transition from welfare into full-time work or seeking increased working hours. The proposed solution centres on substantially raising the tax-free threshold and replacing complex family payments with simple, universal, non-means-tested tax credits for children. Such changes would drastically reduce EMTRs for the target group, making work financially worthwhile, increasing labour supply, and improving overall social mobility.

Introduction

The current tax system is widely perceived as unfair, but the debate often wrongly focuses on whether the wealthy are paying enough. The real challenge for policymakers is ensuring that the system promotes social mobility and rewards effort, particularly for those on low and modest incomes. The existing structure creates a strong disincentive for those on welfare to take up a job or for part-time workers to increase their hours, as the financial gain is minimal. The core aim of the proposed reform is to restore the principle that work should pay better than welfare, requiring a unified approach to tax and social security policy.

Is Australia a 'low tax' country?

The conventional wisdom that Australia is a 'low tax' country is often based on comparing total tax revenue as a percentage of Gross Domestic Product (GDP) with the OECD average. While this metric places Australia in the lower third, it is misleading. The key issue is not the total quantum of tax revenue, but rather the structure of the tax-transfer system and how quickly taxes begin to bite at the bottom of the income scale. The relatively high reliance on income tax in Australia, combined with the way means-tested benefits are withdrawn, creates a problem of high marginal rates that disproportionately impacts low and average earners, thus obscuring the true tax burden felt by these groups.

Should higher income earners pay more tax?

The common political demand to increase taxes on higher income earners to fund services is politically popular but economically questionable. The problem of equity in the Australian system is not predominantly found at the top end. While high marginal tax rates for the wealthy can lead to disincentives for high-achievers and create opportunities for tax minimisation, the most severe disincentives to work and earn more are concentrated at the lower and middle-income levels. The reform should therefore focus on improving incentives for the less well-off rather than increasing the burden on the rich, which may not yield the expected revenue and could encourage capital flight.

Are average earners over-taxed?

In an effective sense, many average earners are indeed over-taxed. A worker on the median wage faces a marginal tax rate of 30% on top of a 1.5% Medicare levy. Furthermore, for those with dependent children or who receive other benefits, the withdrawal of means-tested payments adds significantly to this burden. The combination of income tax and the clawback of family benefits means that a substantial portion of any additional income is lost, often leaving these families with very little financial gain from increased effort. This tax-welfare squeeze is a central theme of the argument for fundamental reform.

The tax-welfare squeeze and the problem of disincentives

The primary disincentive to work is the interaction between the income tax system and the social security system. The means-testing of many welfare payments, such as Family Tax Benefit and various supplementary payments, involves a significant reduction in the benefit amount for every extra dollar earned above a certain threshold. When this benefit withdrawal rate is combined with the statutory income tax rate (e.g., 17% or 30%) and the Medicare levy (1.5%), the result is an EMTR that can easily reach 60% to 80%, making the effort to earn more or move into work financially irrational.

The problem of high Effective Marginal Tax Rates

Effective Marginal Tax Rates (EMTRs) represent the percentage of an extra unit of income lost to tax and benefit withdrawal. These high EMTRs are the single most significant barrier to achieving a 'Make Work Pay' policy. For many Australians on the lower rungs of the income scale, their EMTRs are significantly higher than those faced by the country's top earners. This structural flaw fundamentally undermines the principle of rewarding effort. It traps people in poverty or low-paid, part-time work, acting as a clear economic and social disincentive against self-reliance and increased labour supply.

Problems in making work pay

i. Changing the welfare rules

Attempting to solve the high EMTR problem solely by adjusting welfare means-test rules is problematic. While softening benefit withdrawal rates could help, it would drastically increase the number of people eligible for benefits and would be extremely costly. Furthermore, making small adjustments often just shifts the high EMTR problem to a different point on the income scale, rather than eliminating it. Any approach must be simplified and integrated to be effective.

ii. Changing the tax rules by introducing an 'Earning Credit'

An 'Earning Credit' would be a tax credit designed to be paid to low-income workers and then phased out very slowly as income rises. While this would successfully lower EMTRs, it can be complex to administer and still interacts with the welfare system, potentially creating new pinch points. It is a partial solution that risks adding another layer of complexity to an already opaque system.

iii. Tackling tax and welfare together by raising the zero-rate threshold

The most effective, comprehensive, and transparent reform is to raise the tax-free threshold substantially. This simple change achieves several goals simultaneously: it removes the statutory tax burden for all low-income earners, reduces the number of people who fall into the tax net, and, crucially, creates a significantly wider buffer zone of tax-free income. This expanded buffer would mean that means-tested benefits are withdrawn against a higher net income, reducing the likelihood of a high EMTR 'stacking' effect and immediately rewarding the movement from welfare to work.

Universal non-means-tested tax credits for dependent children

To further simplify the system and address poverty traps affecting families, the existing complex, means-tested family payments should be replaced with a universal, non-means-tested tax credit for each dependent child. This change would eliminate one of the largest contributors to the high EMTR problem — the withdrawal of Family Tax Benefits. A fixed, simple credit would ensure that every working family with children benefits, regardless of income, thus removing a major disincentive to earning more and making the tax liability more transparent.

How much would it 'cost' and can Treasury 'afford' it?

The initial outlay for such a comprehensive reform, particularly raising the tax-free threshold, would be significant, running into billions of dollars of forgone tax revenue. However, the paper argues that this is not a cost but a strategically vital investment. The long-term economic benefits, including increased labour force participation, greater productivity, and reduced reliance on welfare payments, would eventually offset the initial budgetary expense. Furthermore, the enhanced fairness and transparency of the system would justify the outlay, ensuring that the Treasury can and should afford this key structural reform.

Who gains and who loses?

The reform is designed to be highly progressive, improving the financial position of the most vulnerable without significantly disadvantaging those on high incomes.

Full-time workers

Full-time workers on low to middle incomes would experience a significant net gain, benefiting fully from the substantial increase in the tax-free threshold. They would keep a much larger proportion of their earnings compared to the existing system, directly rewarding their labour and improving their standard of living.

Workers who are also on benefits

This group, which includes many part-time or casual workers and single parents, is the primary target and would benefit the most. The combination of a higher tax-free threshold and universal child credits (where applicable) would drastically reduce their EMTRs. This would ensure that for every extra hour worked, they retain a meaningful financial gain, thereby providing the necessary incentive to increase their work effort.

Welfare claimants with no other source of income

The fundamental entitlement of welfare claimants with no other income source would remain protected and not be reduced. The reform focuses on incentivising work and improving the financial returns to labour, not on making the baseline welfare safety net less generous. Therefore, this group would not be made worse off and would benefit immensely from the opportunity to take up work with minimal financial penalty.

This is a summary of a 2004 Centre for Independent Studies research paper. The full paper can be found at https://www.cis.org.au/publication/tax-reform-to-make-work-pay/

Taming the Monster: Reforming Personal Income Tax

Robert Carling (2016)

Without any change in personal income tax rates or thresholds, the average tax rate (net tax paid as a percentage of taxable income) will reach the previous recorded peak and then keep rising to an unprecedented 26.6% within five years, well above the long-term average. In addition:

- Full-time workers on the minimum wage will face a marginal rate of 34.5% (including Medicare levy) and an effective marginal rate of 36% (also including LITO phase-out).

- Adult full-time workers on average earnings will face a marginal rate of 39%.

- The proportion of taxpayers facing either the highest (47%) or second highest (39%) marginal rate will exceed 35%.

The adverse economic impact of personal income tax is already high and is set to rise further if these trends go unchecked. Increasing the thresholds for some or all marginal tax rates to match past growth in average earnings would alleviate the effects of bracket creep. While this has been the typical policy response in the past, it is a band-aid rather than a reform.

Genuine reform would include cuts in marginal rates — including the top rate — and automatic indexation of thresholds to prevent future bracket creep. This approach would provide a long-run supply-side boost to economic growth.

Concerns about the 'fairness' of such an approach are misplaced. Personal income tax (and the tax/transfer system more broadly) is already highly progressive and the trend has been for personal income tax to become more, not less, progressive — notwithstanding tax cuts since the 1990s. Reforms that make the system less progressive should be considered if there is a clear economic pay-off.

Cuts in marginal rates must be reconciled with budget repair. Even a medium size tax cut faces this dilemma. It is best resolved by more disciplined management of public expenditure. Within the tax system, revenue to help finance cuts in marginal rates could be generated by broadening the tax base, but in each case (such as negative gearing, superannuation concessions, capital gains tax and deductions for work-related expenses) there are tight limits to how far the government should sensibly go.

Another way to help accommodate lower marginal rates within the budget constraint would be to abolish the tax-free threshold, which is very costly to revenue, and replace it with tax credits or offsets that phase out at middle incomes.

Calibrating tax cuts

There have been tax cuts of all sizes since the 1970s, ranging from the 'sandwich and milkshake' cut of 2003 up to the large cut of 14% associated with the introduction of the GST in 2000.

- A 'sandwich and milkshake' cut would be about $10 per week per taxpayer on average. The cost to revenue would be about $5 billion a year.

- Moving up the scale, a medium size cut by past standards would be about $25 a week on average. For example, this would be the benefit of correcting for bracket creep since 2012-13 (the last year there was any change), which the CIS estimates would cut revenue by $12.5 billion in 2017/18. However, the average tax rate would still be above the long-term average.

- Reducing the average tax rate to the long-term average would cut revenue by about $19 billion in 2017-18. This would be an average cut of $36 per week per taxpayer.

- A large reduction by past standards would, for example, match the 2000 cut that accompanied introduction of the GST. This would initially cost $30 billion a year and lower the average tax rate below the long-term average to 21.2%. This would be an average cut per taxpayer of $57 per week.

Large reductions would be desirable, and the economic benefits in the form of faster growth would lower the revenue cost over time. However, managing large losses of revenue in the short-term within overall budget constraints would be a challenge to government, requiring significant additional revenue from other sources and/or stronger expenditure restraint than has been evident in recent years.

There is nothing 'fair' about making the rich pay more tax

The personal income tax system is highly progressive (or 'redistributive') and has become more so since the 1990s. The share of income tax paid by the top 20% of taxpayers is over 60% and has been increasing at a faster rate than their share of taxable income. The top 20% pay income tax at a rate of 1.35 times their share of income. The bottom 20% pay tax at less than 0.3 times their share of income. It is hard to sustain an argument that the rich are not paying their 'fair share'.

Don't fiddle with thresholds

Income tax relief can be provided by increasing marginal rate thresholds or by cutting the marginal rates. Over the past 20 years there have been large increases in thresholds but not much reduction in marginal rates. Increases in thresholds tend to be overtaken by growth in average incomes over time and are a band-aid rather than a reform. The benefit to taxpayers is temporary. The best solution is automatic indexation of thresholds to average weekly earnings every year. Cutting marginal rates is preferable because the effect is more enduring and marginal rates are a strong influence on peoples' decisions regarding work, saving and investment.

Key long-term targets for reform

- The long-term goal should be to reduce marginal rates, with a top marginal rate of no more than 35%.
- Thresholds should be automatically indexed to average weekly earnings every year to prevent future bracket creep.
- Consideration should be given to abolishing the tax-free threshold and replacing it with a low income tax offset to help fund cuts in marginal rates.

This is a summary of a 2016 Centre for Independent Studies research paper. The full paper can be found at https://www.cis.org.au/publication/taming-the-monster-reforming-personal-income-tax-2/

The Very Idea of a Flat Tax

Lauchlan Chipman (2004)

The paper sets out to challenge the long-held assumption that progressive taxation is inherently the fairest system. It argues for the moral case for a flat income tax, maintaining that the progressive system, which takes a proportionately larger share of income as earnings rise, cannot be defended on grounds of justice. A flat tax, where all individuals pay the same proportion of their income, is neither progressive nor regressive; it is even-handed and therefore more just. This proportional approach is consistent with the fundamental principle of the Rule of Law, which dictates that like cases should be treated alike, while unlike cases are treated in a way that is proportional to their relevant differences. Thinkers such as J.R. McCulloch and F.A. Hayek are quoted to frame the argument, with Hayek criticising progressive taxation as a discriminatory burden that elevates into a principle that has "no better basis than envy".

Preliminaries

Taxation policy operates at a unique intersection of economics and philosophy, involving debates over empirical questions, such as the effect of incentives and disincentives on human behaviour, and purely philosophical questions concerning ethics, justice, and desirable social goods. Arguments about the desirable outcomes of tax policies are ultimately philosophical, with tenets concerning equity, equality, and justice moving to the centre of the stage. For instance, those who regard material equality as a desirable goal will favour progressive taxation as a key mechanism for state-mandated redistribution. However, this focus on material equality is a philosophically contentious and ultimately indefensible position.

The discussion operates on the assumption that state taxation of personal income is morally legitimate, but it is stressed that all taxation, by its nature, involves the forcible removal of private property and thus requires a morally compelling justification. This is because it imposes a law which necessarily overrides the prior legal rights of the taxpayer. Historically, this has been a point of contention, with Adam Smith strongly opposing a direct income tax because it required an "inquisition of each taxpayer" and could adversely affect capital formation. The ensuing arguments are concerned solely with the principles of personal income taxation, not the specific rates, which are dependent on total state revenue requirements and other forms of taxation.

Flat, Proportional, and Progressive Taxes.

The popular appeal for a flat tax is actually a call for a constant proportional rate of income taxation. This model ensures high earners pay more in amount but rejects the idea that they should pay a higher proportion of their income. A single proportional rate offers clear practical advantages, including enhanced simplicity and transparency, leading to lower administration costs for both the taxpayer and tax collector. Crucially, it also reduces the incentive to create or embrace schemes to conceal income and avoid higher marginal rates.

The argument that higher marginal rates are a disincentive to effort for highly skilled individuals is countered by the observation that they may instead be an incentive for them to work harder to secure a real rise in take-home pay. As different people respond differently, definitive claims about incentives are acknowledged as difficult. A more compelling practical argument against progressive rates is the concept that they are "washed out" by the remuneration system. Wage and salary agreements are typically negotiated with regard to take-home pay. This practice inflates the gross salaries paid to highly remunerated employees, which increases the employer's cost of payroll. Since business costs are reflected in prices, consumers ultimately bear the burden, meaning the progressive income tax on high earners morphs imperceptibly into a flat consumption tax paid by all consumers. This mechanism defeats the intended equalising effects of progressive taxation.

It is also shown that a flat tax is still progressive in impact if it retains a tax-free threshold (personal allowance). If the flat rate is applied only to taxable income above this threshold, the proportion of a person's total income paid in tax will gradually increase as their total income rises, exhibiting a smoother form of progressivism than the bracketed system. However, for pure proportionality, the only option is to abolish the tax-free threshold.

A Flat Tax and Vertical Equity

A just and fair income tax system must encompass both horizontal equity (taxpayers in comparable circumstances taxed comparably) and vertical equity (equity through the range of low to high incomes). Both forms are founded on the ancient principle of procedural justice. The paper contends that a flat proportional rate is the arithmetically perfect mechanism for achieving vertical equity because it treats the difference in income size in a perfectly proportional manner.

Is Every Earned Dollar of Equal Value?

One of the main arguments against the flat tax is the concept of declining marginal utility, which claims that the value of each dollar is not equal for every earner. The argument is that an equal proportional tax would result in a greater sacrifice for a low-income earner, who would "miss the last dollar" more than a high-income earner. The paper reviews and dismisses this as a valid basis for rejecting the flat tax, concluding that the argument does not successfully demonstrate that the flat proportionate rate violates the requirement of procedural justice.

Conclusion

Progressivism in income tax rates violates the fundamental demands of justice, while the flat proportionate rate aligns perfectly with the requirements of procedural justice. The paper rejects the idea that procedural justice should be overridden by a requirement of social justice, particularly in relation to distributive wealth. A flat tax is neither progressive nor regressive, but rather perfectly just. The introduction of a flat tax faces significant political resistance, often being wrongly dismissed as regressive. A practical transition would likely require a comprehensive review of all taxation to mitigate the unacceptable political optics of increasing the tax rate for lower-to-middle income earners while providing large savings for the highest earners. Despite these challenges, the jurisprudential merits of a just system make the move toward a flat tax an imperative.

This is a summary of a 2004 Centre for Independent Studies research paper. The full paper can be found at https://www.cis.org.au/publication/the-very-idea-of-a-flat-tax/

Exposing the Stealth Tax: The bracket Creep Rip-off

Robert Carling and Michael Potter (2015)

Many commentators are calling for additional revenue to be raised to provide funding for current and additional government spending.

There are many arguments against increasing personal taxes. Most importantly, they are inefficient taxes that have substantial harmful impacts on work, saving, investment and growth. But also no clear case has been made to increase taxes instead of curbing spending growth.

One of the ways income taxes are often raised is through bracket creep, also known as fiscal drag, when average tax rates rise automatically in an economy with inflation and growing wages. Our paper shows bracket creep is causing substantial tax increases and as a result is acting as a drag on the economy.

As the government's Re:think discussion paper noted, Australia relies more on income taxes than most other developed (OECD) countries. This causes our tax system to be more inefficient, because income taxes have more adverse effects than many other taxes. It also means that bracket creep has a greater impact in Australia than in other countries.

Importantly, bracket creep isn't just inefficient; the paper demonstrates it also is regressive because it disproportionately hits low- to middle-income earners. The excuses not to fix bracket creep multiply as the demands for increased government spending continue and a number of spending commitments, such as the National Disability Insurance Scheme (NDIS), are locked in. However, the consequences of ignoring bracket creep are severe. Fixing bracket creep must be a serious priority for all politicians.

Weaker budget discipline

Bracket creep makes it easier for governments to increase taxation in a non-transparent way either to finance higher government spending or to reduce a deficit. With tax revenue growing faster than income growth, bracket creep facilitates growth of expenditure and makes it easier for governments to avoid the hard task of expenditure restraint. Th tax increase is providing substantial funding for higher spending. Therefore, bracket creep is supporting the lack of spending discipline.

Without bracket creep, governments would need to apply tighter curbs to spending (CIS' preferred approach) or turn to alternative and perhaps less inefficient revenue sources.

Two arguments are sometimes used against indexation of tax thresholds to address bracket creep:

- Indexation reduces the government's "Budget flexibility to respond to changed economic circumstances". The Henry Tax Review's Consultation Paper mounted a similar argument.
- Bracket creep should be used to help reduce chronic budget deficits.

These views are misguided, as they ignore the substantial costs of bracket creep noted elsewhere in this paper. Budget flexibility or repair are not appropriate reasons for a regressive tax increase that causes an increase in marginal tax rates for 2.5 million Australians.

In addition, the same results (flexibility and budget repair) could be achieved with greater transparency through explicit tax increases or, preferably, expenditure cuts. Moreover, the contribution of bracket creep to flexibility and budget repair is illusory to the extent that bracket creep is used for higher government spending. And this is in fact what is happening now. The tax-to-GDP ratio is around historical averages and set to go well above this ratio. Therefore, it is clear that most, if not all, of the deficit is due to spending increases rather than a revenue shortfall, and bracket creep is (partly) funding this spending. Similarly, the lack of budget flexibility at the moment is due to spending increases.

If governments wish to have budget flexibility or reduce deficits, they should preferably explore spending restraint, rather than using the inefficient and inequitable tax increase through bracket creep.

Consistent budget treatment of inflation

Indexation is common in government budgeting. In fact, not indexing personal tax brackets is glaringly inconsistent with the current practice of indexing fuel and alcohol excise duties for inflation, and indexing tobacco excise to wages growth. Excise indexation is designed to ensure that real revenue doesn't fall due to inflation, while income tax bracket creep acts to *increase* the real value of revenue. In effect, the government is saying to the taxpayer: "heads you lose, tails I win."

There are many other areas where inflation impacts on income tax. For example, inflation increases the effective rate of tax on interest income and the effective deduction for interest expenses. These impacts offset to some extent. In addition, inflation increases the effective tax on capital gains and reduces the effect of depreciation allowances. These impacts are (partly or fully) addressed by the reduced taxes of capital gains, and accelerated depreciation (expensing) for assets.

Inflation affects other federal taxes, such as the GST and company tax. However, the relative size of the personal tax take, and the significant progressivity of the income tax system, means it is likely that the inflationary effects are small for taxes other than personal tax.

The combination of these above factors, particularly bracket creep, means that total revenue grows faster than inflation, and the tax-to-GDP ratio increases, if nothing is done. This is in fact what is currently occurring, and forecast to occur in coming years.

On the spending side, there are a variety of approaches but in general terms, government payments per person or per service are usually indexed to a measure of cost, price or wages.

The conclusion is that indexation is found in most areas of government taxation and spending—and the largest exception is personal taxes, which seem excluded for largely political reasons. It therefore cannot be argued that personal taxes are just one of many parts of the budget that aren't adjusted for inflation. In any case, failure to address inflation/wages growth in any other area of the budget is a poor reason for failing to act on bracket creep.

Impact on fiscal stabilisation

It is argued that bracket creep may assist the budget with stabilisation of the economy. When the economy is booming, tax revenues increase quickly, cooling the economy; and taxes rise more slowly when economic growth is sluggish—bracket creep even delivers an effective tax cut if there is deflation. These automatic stabilisers are often considered to be a desirable feature of budgets as they automatically reduce the scale of the business cycle and avoid some of the disadvantages of discretionary fiscal stabilisation policies, such as implementation lags. Indexation would, at the margin, weaken the automatic stabilisers.

However, automatic stabilisers still work without bracket creep, as the government budget balance is still counter-cyclical. In particular, unemployment benefits grow strongly in a downturn, and tax receipts grow naturally in an upturn because of increased employment.

In addition, some research indicates that bracket creep can operate in exactly the opposite direction: it can drive increases in inflation if workers and their unions push for higher wages to compensate for the tax increase caused by bracket creep. This would lead to an overheating economy becoming even more overheated. Ultimately, however, the sustainability of inflation driven by higher costs depends on monetary policy accommodation.

But more importantly, the benefits of fiscal stabilisers are greatly overstated. The impact of the government budget balance on the whole economy is muted in an economy such as Australia with a floating dollar and an open capital market, meaning that automatic fiscal stabilisers also have a limited impact. By contrast, monetary policy has a strong impact on the economy.

There are also better approaches to deal with an overheating economy than to rely on bracket creep—in particular it is better to increase the supply of labour and capital and open the economy up to competition.

Government accountability and transparency

Bracket creep results in taxpayers facing an increase in tax rates due to inflation and real wages growth with no action from governments. This feature has earned it the popular label of a 'stealth tax'. The increase takes the form of an increase in effective rather than statutory (or 'headline') tax rates. If legislators had to pass legislation to achieve the same revenue increase, it is likely that they would think twice about doing so.

The attraction of an automatic increase in revenue is political in that it comes without the attention and difficulty of legislation. Moreover, tax increases may be difficult to pass in the Federal Parliament, in which the government usually lacks an upper house majority. By contrast, the parliament is not an obstacle to bracket creep, because bracket creep results from legislative *in*action.

Bracket creep detracts from transparency, which is a healthy feature of a democracy. Individual taxpayers may not notice the effect of bracket creep on their own tax payments because it happens without publicity and the cost per year is small, although the cumulative impact is much larger as shown in the modelling results above. As a result, it promotes the illusion that taxes are lower than they actually are.

The additional revenue from bracket creep can also facilitate deceptive tax trade-offs. For example, after a period of bracket creep, a government may announce cuts in income tax in exchange for an increase in indirect tax—when in fact the income tax cuts are merely returning the proceeds of bracket creep.

Even if there isn't a trade-off with increases in other taxes, bracket creep still works against transparency. Governments have managed bracket creep through periodic discretionary tax cuts. These tax 'cuts' are a fiscal illusion; they have often been nothing more than handing back the proceeds of cumulative bracket creep that would never have occurred in the first place had thresholds been appropriately indexed.

Similarly, politicians see a political advantage in bracket creep in that they prefer making specific announcements of large, discrete tax cuts instead of allowing smaller, annual, automatic cuts that would result from annual indexation.

Automatic indexation does not rule out discretionary tax changes, either up or down. It creates a more meaningful and transparent starting point for such discretionary adjustments and makes it clear that the adjustments are either genuine tax increases or tax cuts.

Solutions to bracket creep

Personal income tax bracket creep could easily be stopped by applying automatic indexation to tax thresholds, similar to the indexation governments have eagerly applied to excise and pensions.

Indexation of tax thresholds to inflation would deal with a substantial part of bracket creep, but not all of it—real bracket creep would not be addressed. Taxpayers would still face tax increases if they receive any real wage increase, which would cause numerous problems including:

- an ever-increasing tax-to-GDP ratio;
- tax increases for people receiving a below average wage increase; and
- the imposition of a regressive and inequitable tax increase will still occur.

As a consequence, bracket creep is only being fully addressed if tax thresholds are indexed to growth in income or wages. If this occurs, taxpayers who receive an average real wage increase will still be required to share this with the government; they just won't be forced to share *more than a proportionate* amount with government. The tax rate will go up for those receiving an above average wage increase and will go down for those earning a below average wage increase. This is a fairer approach, closer to the intent of a progressive income tax system. Nevertheless, indexation to inflation is better than no indexation at all.

Ideally, tax thresholds should be indexed to growth in taxable income. However, there is no timely index for growth in this measure. Growth in average wages would serve as a reasonable proxy and has been used in the modelling in this paper. Other options for indexation include growth in nominal GDP or nominal national income. The benefit of these indexation factors is that they would deal with bracket creep that occurs if taxable income grows more quickly than real wages—and modelling for this paper indicates that this is currently occurring. Of course, there is scope for governments to use discretionary tax adjustments to deal with taxable income growing faster than wages, but there are many disadvantages with a discretionary approach, as noted below.

Whatever the chosen index is, it should be clearly specified, published by an independent authority such as the Australian Bureau of Statistics, and not subject to government adjustment or discretion, as supported by the historical Australian evidence and the international evidence explored below.

The extent of bracket creep will also be reduced if marginal tax rates are lower, since bracket creep has a greater impact when average tax rates increase more quickly—and the way to limit this increase is to have lower marginal tax rates. The CIS has long advocated lower marginal tax rates, noting that the distortions and inefficiencies from the tax system are smaller if marginal rates are reduced.

Conclusion

Bracket creep is a tax increase that affects all taxpayers in Australia—though it hits low- and middle-income earners the hardest — and is more severe when inflation and real wages growth is higher. There is very little to be said in favour of bracket creep. It is not helping to plug a revenue gap; instead it is being used to finance increased spending, when there are clear benefits for spending restraint to be used to return the budget to balance. The evidence to date is that governments misuse the flexibility given them by bracket creep to use this as a stealth tax increase. Bracket creep also allows governments to provide illusory tax cuts that are merely a refund of overpaid tax.

To the extent bracket creep works as an automatic stabilizer, it is a clearly inferior way to stabilise the economy; there are much better ways to do that.

All the supposed benefits of bracket creep ignore its harmful effects, including reducing employment, innovation, productivity and economic growth. They also ignore the disproportionate harm bracket creep causes for low- and middle-income earners.

The indexation of tax thresholds will address this issue. Tax thresholds should be indexed to a measure of income growth or set at a particular proportion of average wages. This will stop bracket creep and its harmful effects on the economy and society.

This is an edited extract of a 2015 Centre for Independent Studies research paper published in 2015. The full paper can be found at https://www.cis.org.au/publication/exposing-the-stealth-tax-the-bracket-creep-rip-off-2/

Indexation would end the Stealth Tax of Bracket Creep

Gene Tunny (2025)

In Australia, bracket creep has become a silent but significant burden on taxpayers, eroding real take-home pay and fuelling the growth of government revenue without explicit consent.

Bracket creep occurs when inflation pushes nominal wages into higher tax brackets, even though real incomes may not have increased. For example, consider somebody earning just under $135,000 who receives a pay rise of 2.5% that merely compensates her for inflation over the year. She previously had to pay 30 cents of tax on every extra dollar she earns but now has to pay 37 cents. The nominal income boost she received to compensate her for the cost of living increase is taxed at a higher marginal tax rate than before, even though she is not better off in real terms. Her average tax rate is higher and she is worse off in real terms.

Axing this hidden tax would not only give relief to taxpayers but allow for real reform that would allow political parties to fulfil their promises to lower taxes. This could be done by indexing income tax thresholds to inflation, such as the Consumer Price Index (CPI). If the threshold for the 37% marginal tax rate were inflation-adjusted to $138,375, she would not end up paying 37% in tax on her additional earnings.

Because tax thresholds are fixed in nominal terms, inflation gradually pushes more of each pay rise into higher tax brackets. For example, if an individual's salary increases by 2-3% to keep pace with inflation, but the tax brackets remain unchanged, a larger portion of their income is taxed at a higher rate. Over time, this results in an automatic increase in the average tax rate, even though the taxpayer's real income — their purchasing power — has not improved.

This process is how bracket creep effectively acts as a hidden tax, silently increasing the government's revenue without the need for explicit tax rate hikes. As a result, the tax-to-GDP ratio rises, enabling the government to finance an ever-expanding public sector. While this may seem beneficial for funding public services, it comes at the cost of reduced disposable income for households and adverse implications for productivity.

When taxpayers have less money to spend or invest, consumer demand and private sector growth are stifled, ultimately harming the broader economy. Bracket creep does not affect all taxpayers equally. Research by the Centre for Independent Studies highlights that, while higher-income individuals pay more in absolute tax dollars, bracket creep disproportionately raises tax rates for those in the early stages of their careers or on lower incomes.

For younger workers, nominal wage increases — often intended merely to keep pace with cost-of-living pressures — can push them into higher tax brackets faster. This means that even modest pay rises, which do not reflect real income growth, can result in a higher tax burden.

Governments occasionally attempt to address bracket creep by announcing tax cuts every few years. But these measures only provide temporary relief. Indeed, the Parliamentary Budget Office found that the effects of the Stage 3 tax cuts would be offset by bracket creep by the end of the decade. By linking thresholds to inflation, tax rates would only increase when real incomes grow, rather than automatically rising due to nominal wage increases that merely match inflation. This would ensure that taxpayers are not penalised for wage increases that merely match cost-of-living increases and that the tax system remains fair and transparent.

Indexation would provide greater certainty for taxpayers and policymakers alike. Households could better plan their finances without fearing that inflation would erode their take-home pay, while governments would have to justify the increases in the tax burden that bracket creep brings about covertly.

This shift would foster a more honest and productive debate about tax policy, focusing on real reforms rather than the occasional giving back of additional taxes raised through bracket creep in politically-timed tax cuts.

Indexing tax thresholds would not only end bracket creep but could be a key part of broader tax reform. For example, indexation could be combined with measures to simplify the tax system, reduce marginal tax rates, or provide targeted relief for low- and middle-income earners. This would enhance economic efficiency, promote workforce participation, and support long-term growth.

It's time for Australia to take this simple yet transformative step toward a fairer and more sustainable tax system.

This opinion piece was originally published in 2025 by the *Australian Financial Review.*

Fix it or fail:
Why We Must Cut Company Tax Now

Michael Potter (2006)

The Australian economy has major structural weaknesses. And if we fail to fix these weaknesses, the risk is that wages, incomes, productivity and GDP stagnate.

Business investment is at near-record lows. It has been lower only once: in the depths of the 1990s recession. Mining investment is plummeting and is not being replaced by non-mining investment. There is an enormou amount of global capital, but it isn't going to Australian business investment. Productivity growth is weak and national income growth is near zero. Wages growth is at or near record low levels.

Australia's economic growth rate cannot be sustained without boosting investment and productivity. These are the only ways we can get sustained growth in household incomes given we are expecting long-term declines in labour force participation.

Australia's company tax (30 per cent) is very uncompetitive. Our company tax rate is above OECD averages, particularly when taking account of the size of our economy. Australia's tax rate is well above what should be expected for a country of our size.

Almost all OECD countries have cut their corporate tax rate since 2001: the average decline is 6 7 percentage points. In contrast Australia's rate has remained unchanged. If trends continue, our tax rate will still be above the average even after the proposed company tax cut is fully implemented. Australian companies pay more tax than OECD averages. This holds even when dividend imputation and the proposed tax cut are subtracted.

Cutting company tax is one of the best ways to address our economy's underlying weaknesses. The tax cut will encourage more investment into Australian businesses, particularly from foreign investors.

Increased investment will expand the economy, resulting in a sizable boost to incomes and wages. There is widespread agreement that higher investment will expand the economy, as well as promoting competition, productivity and access to innovative technology.

The detailed modelling by Treasury agrees: GDP is set to increase by over 1%, a substantial increase as argued by Treasury. It is around the same benefit as wide-ranging reforms in the 1990s. The gain to wages after tax is expected to be about 1.1%, and household incomes around 0.7%, given the measure need not be funded by personal tax increases or bracket creep. The tax cut is expected to increase productivity by up to 1%: a half year's productivity growth will come from this policy alone. This is consistent with the uniform agreement by experts that company tax is the most inefficient tax levied by the federal government. Cutting this tax will make the economy more productive. These results are supported by numerous studies of international evidence.

The modelling likely underestimates the benefits of the tax cut, because it assumes companies don't increase locally-financed investment. The modelling assumes that imputation nullifies the effect of company tax on Australians, but this doesn't accord with market valuations or company behaviour.

Other arguments for a company tax cut include:

- Company tax revenue is becoming very reliant on a small number of taxpayers, so the budget is highly exposed to the risks of these individual companies. A tax cut will ease this reliance.
- Company tax is like a tariff on imported capital and should be reformed like these other tariffs. Just as with tariff reforms, the decision to implement the tax cut should be based on the benefit to the whole economy.
- The tax cut provides tax reductions to all businesses, not just small business, and there are reasons to expect larger businesses to provide the greater economic benefit. Larger businesses have, on average, recently

experienced improved profitability, productivity and employment, and provide more workplace flexibility.

- The budget impact of the tax cut is small or zero, given other recent measures to broaden the tax base.
- The economic growth generated by the tax cut will result in an offsetting increase in tax revenue, significantly reducing the costs of the tax cut — and the offset is likely to be larger if the underestimate of investment response is corrected.

Without a tax cut, the overall tax burden will reach an all-time high in a decade, based on current forecasts. The tax cut need not be phased in over 10 years. Australia needs a boost to investment, productivity and wages today. However, it is better for the tax cut to be phased in than for it to be cancelled completely. The phase-in will encourage investment to increase before the tax cuts are fully implemented — but only if the tax cuts are 'locked in'.

Company tax mythbuster

- Myth: companies shouldn't get a tax cut because there is so much tax avoidance

Companies paying full taxes have nothing to do with supposed tax avoiders. The taxpaying companies shouldn't be penalised for actions of unrelated companies. Collective responsibility for the 'sins' of others is an anathema to good public policy.

Australian companies pay much more tax than the OECD average and the ATO says there isn't evidence of widespread tax avoidance. Nevertheless, cancelling the tax cut encourages an increase in tax avoidance. Many actions are being taken to address tax avoidance and the funds raised by this are helping pay for the company tax cut.

- Myth: the benefits of the tax cut are small compared to the costs

Treasury has argued the benefits are substantial; they are similar to the gains from the major infrastructure reforms in the 1990s — these gains aren't being criticised as being 'too small'. The Treasury modelling indicates sizable gains to GDP, wages, incomes, investment and productivity after costs are subtracted. These gains are supported by detailed studies of international evidence published in highly regarded journals.

The benefits are underestimated. The modelling assumes that the only benefit to investment comes from foreigners, when in fact Australian financed investment is likely to grow as well.

- Myth: The benefits round to zero

On the same basis, the cost to revenue rounds to zero as well. Better analysis indicates the tax cut should make GDP and wages higher each and every year for the rest of time, even after the costs are subtracted.

- Myth: the funds for the tax cut should be spent on education or other policies

The tax cut can be fully funded from the tax increases in the 2016–17 Budget, so it doesn't preclude any other policy from happening. The policy has large benefits relative to costs; other policies should go ahead if they can similarly demonstrate benefits much larger than costs.

- Myth: The tax cut isn't worth doing because the costs occur now and the benefits are delayed

The same argument could be used against investment in infrastructure or education

- Myth: the tax cut provides a big windfall to foreigners/big business

Treasury finds that most of the benefit will ultimately go to workers. In the longer term, the benefits to foreign investors and the US Treasury will be small. The policy generates considerable benefits to Australians; any benefits to foreigners should be seen as a bonus. Benefits to foreigners should increase the support for a policy, just as collateral damage to foreigners should reduce support.

- Myth: the tax cut will cause national income to decrease, based on modelling by Janine Dixon

Dixon's modelling implies foreign investment harms Australia, which is completely contradicted by the evidence. Australia is built on foreign investment. The modelling is of a different policy, not the government's policy. Dixon's modelling, like the Treasury modelling, underestimates the benefit of the tax cut by assuming that Australian financed investment doesn't increase due to a tax cut.

- Myth: the modelling unbelievably assumes that tax avoidance will fall dramatically with the tax cut

This doesn't follow from the Treasury modelling. This modelling is largely unaffected by tax avoidance assumptions. Nevertheless, if tax avoidance is less responsive to tax rates than assumed, then the benefits of the tax cut are likely to be larger not smaller.

- Myth: Imputation means Australia's tax system is competitive

Factoring in the tax cut, as well as dividend imputation, still means the revenue from Australia's company tax is well above OECD averages. Adjusting for imputation is questionable because foreign investors put little or no value on imputation, and foreign investors are most influenced by differences in tax burdens.

This is a summary of a 2006 Centre for Independent Studies research paper. The full paper can be found at https://www.cis.org.au/publication/fix-it-or-fail-why-we-must-cut-company-tax-now/

Right or Rort? Dissecting Australia's Tax Concessions

Robert Carling (2015)

While action is needed to correct structural budget deficits, the criticism of tax concessions has lost sight of the legitimate reasons for many of them, and often overestimates the revenue gain. On the whole, the so-called concessions for capital gains tax, negative gearing, superannuation, dividend imputation, and the goods and services tax are not really concessions at all but legitimate structural features of the tax system, and in some cases are essential to prevent distortions arising from taxation of savings and investment. Tinkering with tax concessions to raise more revenue on its own does not constitute beneficial tax reform.

There is a widespread and mistaken belief that the closure of tax concessions applied to capital gains tax, negative gearing, dividend imputation, superannuation, and GST could contribute tens of billions of dollars to budget deficit reduction with relative ease.

Right or Rort?: Dissecting Australia's Tax Concessions argues that this belief is based on skewed analysis, a misunderstanding of the facts, and a failure to recognise the valid reasons for some (but not all) of the concessions.

Many of what are labelled 'tax expenditures' — lost revenue attributed to tax concessions — are in fact desirable structural features of an efficient and equitable tax system. They are not necessarily 'loopholes' or 'rorts'. A balanced assessment is required to keep tax concessions in proper perspective in the search for budget savings.

Much of the mythology around the potential revenue to be gained from abolishing tax concessions comes from misinterpretation of the Tax Expenditure Statement (TES) published by the Treasury.

The inherent limitations of the TES are often overlooked against the advice of Treasury and the revenue cost of some concessions is greatly exaggerated.

The scope for additional revenue is much narrower than is often suggested, due to:

- imprecision in the estimates;
- the contentiousness of the specified 'benchmark' tax treatment;
- inability of the estimates to account for taxpayer behaviour in response to changes in tax concessions;
- an incorrect assumption that estimates for revenue forgone are equivalent to potential revenue gain; and
- errors arising from aggregating individual estimates that are not independent of each other.

The tax concessions most often targeted for criticism, and which account for the largest portion of the tax expenditure estimates, are capital gains tax, negative gearing, dividend imputation, superannuation, and GST. Each should be assessed on its own merits.

Capital gains tax (CGT)

CGT exemptions and discounts are defensible on the grounds that savings should be taxed more lightly than other income. This is beneficial to investment and competitiveness. There is a stronger case to increase the discount than to decrease or abolish it.

Negative gearing

Deductibility of interest on borrowings for investment purposes is just a specific case of the general principle that expenses incurred to generate an income are deductible for tax purposes. Limiting the deductibility of expenses could be justified only if rent income was taxed concessionally, which it is not.

Dividend imputation

The effect of imputation is to avoid double taxation of dividends as both company and personal income. While some tax experts argue that Australia's integration in global capital markets has diminished the benefits of imputation, and international investment considerations favour a lower company tax rate instead, domestic markets favour retention of imputation. Ideally, both would apply.

Superannuation

With its long-term focus, superannuation is the best example of why saving needs to be taxed at relatively lower rates to avoid tax-induced distortions — a principle widely recognised around the world. Statements made about the huge cost of superannuation tax concessions are based on the comprehensive income tax benchmark, but this is arguably inappropriate.

Goods and Services Tax (GST)

GST concessions are substantial, and removing them could raise as much revenue as increasing the GST rate. However, removing some concessions is not straightforward. In education, health, and medical services, the removal of GST would distort the market, while the removal of GST on uncooked food would raise equity issues.

Tinkering with tax concessions does not constitute beneficial tax reform and is unlikely to yield as much revenue as is often forecast.

If reductions in tax concessions are to be justified, they should form part of a broad, revenue neutral tax reform with off-setting reductions in income tax rates.

This is a summary Snapshot of a 2015 Centre for Independent Studies research paper. The full paper can be found at https://www.cis.org.au/publication/right-or-rort-dissecting-australias-tax-concessions/

Myth vs Reality: The Case Against Increasing Capital Gains Tax

Robert Carling (2019)

Introduction

Australia's capital gains tax (CGT) framework has been largely stable for two decades but re-emerged as a political issue following Labor's 2016 and 2019 proposal to effectively increase the tax by 50%. This paper examines the evolution of CGT, the justifications for past reforms, and whether discounting or indexing capital gains is the better policy. He evaluates arguments for and against adjusting CGT for inflation, explores the revenue implications of reform, and concludes that the case for higher CGT is weak and based on persistent misconceptions.

Evolution of Australia's Capital Gains Tax

Before 1985, Australia lacked a comprehensive CGT. The Hawke government introduced one as part of a broader reform that exchanged a wider tax base for lower personal tax rates. The original CGT applied full marginal rates to **real gains**, with cost bases indexed to the Consumer Price Index (CPI). An *averaging provision* helped smooth out "lumpy" gains that might otherwise push taxpayers into higher brackets.

In 1999, the Howard government replaced indexation with a **50% discount** on nominal gains for assets held over a year, following the Ralph Review of Business Taxation. The averaging provision was abolished, though few critics acknowledge this. Superannuation funds received a smaller, one-third discount to reflect their lower tax rate.

The change was not, as often claimed, a 'halving' of CGT but a shift in how inflation and other investment risks were recognised. A later proposal by the Henry Review (2009) suggested a uniform 40% discount, while Labor's 2016 and 2019 policies aimed to reduce the discount for individuals to 25%, retaining the existing rate for superannuation and small business assets.

How the Reforms Were Justified

1985: CGT was justified on three grounds:

1. Capital gains are a legitimate form of income.
2. Excluding them distorts economic behaviour.
3. Benefits had disproportionately accrued to high-income earners.

At the same time, policymakers recognised that taxing purely inflationary gains would be unfair and that very high marginal rates required offsetting reforms such as the averaging concession.

1999: The Ralph Review argued for discounting not only to simplify the system but also to account for factors beyond inflation, including:

- The disincentive effect of CGT on savings and investment.
- The higher risk of capital gains investments.
- The "lock-in" effect that discouraged asset sales.
- International competitiveness, given lighter CGT burdens overseas.

Thus, the 50% discount was designed to invigorate markets and stimulate investment, not simply to offset inflation.

Current Debate: Modern critics argue that as inflation is now low, the 50% discount is excessive. The paper rebuts this on three counts:

- The discount was never intended purely as inflation compensation.

- Inflation at the time of reform was already low (~2.5%), similar to current levels.

- The discount replaced averaging, meaning it cannot be reduced without restoring that provision.

Labor's argument that the CGT discount drives housing unaffordability and constitutes an "unfair subsidy" ignores the fact that only around 38% of capital gains come from real estate. Moreover, the historical relationship between CGT settings and housing prices is tenuous: booms and slumps have occurred under various tax regimes.

To Discount or to Index?

Both methods have merits.

Indexation precisely removes inflation but is complex, requiring cost-base adjustments for each asset parcel.

Discounting is simpler and can encompass broader policy aims such as encouraging saving and risk-taking. However, its calibration is imprecise.

The paper models inflation at 2.5% and finds:

- **50% discount:** fully compensates for inflation when nominal gains exceed 5% per year.

- **25% discount:** fails to do so until gains exceed 10% per year, meaning most investors would pay tax on inflationary, not real, gains.

Hence, a 25% discount would often be more punitive than the pre-1999 indexation regime.

Should Policy Over- or Under-Compensate for Inflation?

Reasons to Under-Compensate

1. **Realisation Basis:** CGT applies only when gains are realised, effectively deferring taxation and providing a time-based benefit.

2. **Consistency:** Other forms of savings income (e.g. interest) are not inflation-adjusted, but this is a poor justification for further inequity.
3. **Equity:** As higher-income taxpayers realise more gains, critics view CGT concessions as regressive. Yet overall system progressivity already addresses this concern.
4. **Income Switching:** Lower CGT rates may encourage investors to reclassify income or alter portfolios for tax reasons.

Reasons to Over-Compensate

1. **Disincentive Effects:** CGT penalises saving and long-term investment; higher rates deter capital formation and risk-taking.
2. **Bunching of Gains:** Realisation can push taxpayers into higher brackets; a discount mitigates this.
3. **Lock-In Effect:** Taxpayers delay asset sales to avoid tax, reducing market efficiency.
4. **Double Taxation:** CGT can duplicate company tax when gains reflect retained earnings already taxed at the corporate level.

Discounting is the Better Solution

CGT policy involves much more than inflation adjustment. While indexation is exact, discounting better reflects a range of economic and equity considerations and offers simplicity:

- A **25% discount** would under-compensate for inflation in most cases and impose the heaviest CGT burden in Australia's history.
- The **50% discount** aligns more closely with real gains and incorporates non-inflation justifications for concessional treatment.
- A **40% discount**, as proposed by the Henry Review, could be a reasonable compromise.

Discounting also rewards higher real returns and longer holding periods — traits that policymakers often view as desirable. Changes to the discount should consider broader tax rates; since 1999, top marginal rates have barely fallen, so there is no case for cutting the discount further. Labor's policy, by both halving the discount and raising top rates, would lift the effective CGT rate by 56%.

Revenue Considerations

Revenue motives largely drive proposals to reduce the discount. In 2015–16, CGT contributed $11 billion (3% of total tax revenue), with individuals providing $6.5 billion. Treasury's estimate that the discount 'costs' $8 billion in foregone revenue exaggerates potential gains, as taxpayers would alter behaviour — deferring sales or holding assets longer — if the tax rose. The actual gain from Labor's proposal was projected at around $2 billion annually.

Historical data show that after the 1999 reforms, CGT revenue rose as a share of personal income tax, suggesting that the 50% discount **stimulated realisations** rather than eroding revenue. Halving the discount could therefore have the opposite effect by re-tightening the lock-in effect and suppressing asset turnover.

Conclusion

Halving the CGT discount would substantially increase the effective tax burden and risk undermining investment and efficiency. Since no fixed discount can perfectly match inflation, the current system should be seen as a pragmatic compromise recognising multiple economic realities.

There are two preferable policy paths:

1. **Retain the 50% discount**, preserving simplicity and competitiveness.
2. **Reinstate indexation** but apply a modest additional discount (10–20%) to real gains.

This is a summary of a 2019 Centre for Independent Studies research paper. The full paper can be found at https://www.cis.org.au/publication/myth-vs-reality-the-case-against-increasing-capital-gains-tax/

State Taxation and Fiscal Federalism: A Blueprint for Further Reform

Robert Carling (2006)

While state taxation is often overshadowed by Commonwealth taxation, it remains a critical area for reform. State taxes raised about $42 billion in 2004–05 and significantly affect the economy. The introduction of the Goods and Services Tax (GST) in 2000 replaced several inefficient state taxes, but states remain heavily dependent on Commonwealth grants, undermining their fiscal autonomy. The paper reviews the reforms brought by the GST and outlines further steps to modernise and rationalise state taxation while strengthening fiscal federalism.

1. An Overview of State Revenue

Tax revenue forms about one-third of total state revenue, with the remainder coming from Commonwealth grants and other sources. Payroll tax, stamp duties, land tax, gambling taxes, and motor vehicle charges make up the main state taxes. Although all GST revenue is passed to the states, the Australian Bureau of Statistics correctly classifies it as Commonwealth revenue because states cannot determine its rate or base. Commonwealth grants are split between untied general-purpose grants and tied specific-purpose grants, the latter earmarked for functions such as hospitals and schools.

2. State Taxation Before the GST

Before the GST, dissatisfaction with state taxes stemmed from their inefficiency and volatility, particularly stamp duties that distorted business activity. The narrow bases and turnover nature of these taxes imposed high economic costs. Dependence on Commonwealth funding and weak revenue growth further eroded states' fiscal independence. Although payroll tax was criticised as a "tax on jobs," economists viewed it as one of the few broad-based taxes under state control.

3. GST-Related Reforms

The 1999 Intergovernmental Agreement on Commonwealth-State Financial Relations initiated the abolition of several state taxes, including financial institutions duty and debits tax, removing around $3 billion in inefficient taxes. Over time, additional duties on mortgages, leases, and business conveyances were also scheduled for abolition. However, major stamp duties on property, insurance, and motor vehicles remained. Despite concerns about states' reluctance to follow through, the replacement of multiple inefficient taxes by the GST improved the overall efficiency of the national tax system.

4. Remaining Reform Issues

After the GST reforms, around $40 billion in state taxes continued to exist, dominated by payroll tax, land tax, stamp duties, gambling taxes, and vehicle charges. These taxes suffer from narrow bases, complex rate structures, and numerous exemptions that heighten inefficiency. The paper focuses on three of the most significant taxes — payroll tax, land tax, and stamp duty — arguing that each needs substantial reform.

(i) Payroll Tax

Payroll tax is defended by economists as a stable revenue source comparable to income or consumption taxes, though its base has been eroded by exemptions and high thresholds. Currently imposed at 4.75–6.85%, it affects only a small proportion of businesses. A broader base with lower rates would be more efficient, but political resistance has made this unlikely. Abolishing payroll tax would require a higher GST rate and further weaken state autonomy. Instead, the paper recommends harmonising payroll tax definitions and administration among states while preventing further erosion of the base.

(ii) Land Tax

Land tax, theoretically an efficient and immobile base for sub-national governments, has also been undermined by extensive exemptions and progressive rates. Exemptions for owner-occupied and agricultural land narrow the base to a fraction of potential coverage. The paper proposes replacing multiple thresholds and rates with a uniform low rate, integrated with local government rates. However, political opposition — particularly from homeowners — makes reform difficult. A comprehensive, low-rate land tax could work if paired with the abolition of property transfer duty.

(iii) Stamp Duty on Property Transfers

Property transfer duty is a volatile but lucrative revenue source. It taxes property turnover rather than production, leading to housing immobility and inefficient allocation of resources. Its progressive rate structure has produced "bracket creep," sharply raising the effective tax burden over time. Carling calls for its abolition or replacement with a broad-based land tax, which would reduce volatility and economic distortion.

(iv) Stamp Duties on Motor Vehicles and Insurance

These selective turnover taxes are inefficient and duplicative given the GST. Insurance duties, especially when combined with fire service levies, can exceed 50% of premiums in some states. Carling suggests abolishing these taxes and replacing insurance-based levies with property-based ones.

5. Financing Further State Tax Reform

Abolishing the remaining inefficient stamp duties would cost about $14 billion. Carling identifies several options to finance this:

1. **Future Growth of GST Revenue:** States could use future growth in GST revenue to fund reform, but the gains are too small and unevenly distributed.
2. **Increase the GST Rate:** Raising the GST from 10% to about 13–14% could finance full abolition, improving efficiency but increasing vertical fiscal imbalance.
3. **Increase Efficient State Taxes:** Broadening payroll and land tax bases could offset the lost revenue. For example, a 0.4–0.5% levy on all land values could replace transfer duty.
4. **Combination of Measures:** A mix of a modest GST increase, some GST growth allocation, and small payroll or land tax extensions could balance efficiency with political feasibility.

6. Reforming Fiscal Federalism

Australia's vertical fiscal imbalance — where states rely heavily on Commonwealth transfers — is among the highest in the world. The GST reforms failed to fix this imbalance, as states lack control over GST policy. True federalism requires fiscal autonomy: states should bear responsibility for both spending and revenue raising. Excessive dependence on tied Commonwealth grants erodes accountability and blurs responsibilities. To strengthen federalism, there should be a reallocation of revenue powers to states while reducing conditional Commonwealth funding.

7. Restructuring State Revenue

To reduce dependency, several approaches are considered:

- **State Control of GST:** Converting GST to a genuine state tax would improve autonomy but faces constitutional barriers and administrative complexity.
- **Expansion of Existing State Taxes:** Broader payroll and land taxes could raise revenue but offer only limited relief from vertical imbalance.
- **Introduction of New State Taxes:** Within constitutional limits, the most viable option is a state income tax, ideally through a 'piggybacking' arrangement similar to Canada's.

8. A State Income Tax?

The Canadian 'piggybacking' approach — where provinces apply their own rate to the federal tax base administered by a single authority — offers simplicity and flexibility. He recommends a similar system for Australia: states could levy a flat income tax rate, such as 10% on income above the federal threshold, collected by the Australian Taxation Office. This would avoid duplication, ensure transparency, and give states a meaningful fiscal instrument without redefining the tax base. To prevent public sector expansion, the new tax should be offset by equivalent Commonwealth income tax cuts.

9. Tax and Grant Switching Options

The paper proposes specific revenue-neutral 'swaps'. One option would see the Commonwealth retain half the GST revenue, reduce its income tax by about $20 billion, and allow states to impose an equivalent personal income tax. A stronger version would reduce specific purpose payments by $20 billion, further shifting income tax powers to states and dismantling many tied grants. Combined with a modest GST rate rise, this would create a fairer and more autonomous fiscal structure.

10. Bringing It Together – A Blueprint for Reform

The final blueprint combines tax efficiency with fiscal autonomy:

- **Tax Reform:** Abolish remaining stamp duties and insurance levies, financed mainly by lifting the GST to 12.5%. Broaden payroll and land tax bases while keeping rates low.

- **Federal Reform:** Retain 5 percentage points of the GST at Commonwealth level and pass 7.5 points to states. Eliminate most specific-purpose grants. Cut Commonwealth income tax by one-third and allow states to levy matching flat-rate income taxes on the same base.

These reforms would lift states' self-funding ratio to about 75%, aligning

Australia's fiscal balance with federations such as Canada and Germany. While politically challenging, such reforms would enhance accountability, efficiency, and true federalism without expanding government overall.

This is a summary of a 2006 Centre for Independent Studies research paper. The full paper can be found at https://www.cis.org.au/publication/state-taxation-and-fiscal-federalism-a-blueprint-for-further-reform/

NSW needs to lead the charge on reforming GST share-out

Robert Carling (2024)

The carve-up of GST revenue among the states is never likely to be a barbecue stopper (except perhaps in Perth), but it occasionally hits the headlines — as it did thanks to the Commonwealth Grants Commission's (CGC) latest recommendations. There are winners and losers from these updates every year, and this time New South Wales and Queensland are the losers. The NSW Premier is livid, and demanding a shift to states' population shares (equal per capita, or EPC, in the jargon) as the basis for distribution. There is more than a little political posturing in the Premier's stance, as his government struggles with persistent deficits and a heavy debt burden.

The absolute decline in the NSW GST allocation for 2024-25 is no more than a rounding error in its budget, and the CGC has in fact set the NSW share lower in five of the past 20 years. But the GST shortfall relative to expectations is material. This has always been one of the problems with the distribution methodology; predicting what will come out of it is like trying to crack the Enigma code.

Hell hath no fury like a Premier and a Treasurer hearing three months before their budget that plans for a return to operating surpluses after five years of massive deficits have been disrupted by Canberra bureaucrats tweaking the dials of horizontal fiscal equalisation (HFE). There is nothing new in NSW politicians demanding a shift to EPC distribution. They've been at it for decades. Every time they are mugged by the equalisation system, the NSW Treasury dusts off a well-thumbed file of suitable talking points.

This is not to make light of the case for reform. There is much to be said for an equal-per-capita distribution. It would be simple, understandable, predictable, efficient and impervious to gaming. With an adjustment for the uneven interstate distribution of mineral resources and royalties, it could also pass the fairness test. But as Premier Minns and Treasurer Mookhey must know, it is not about to happen — not because the idea lacks merit, but because the current system is entrenched with strong political and institutional support.

The HFE system has been reviewed over the years more times than the tax system, and there has never been an outcome more than tinkering at the edges. The only review to recommend a pathway to EPC was the one conducted by eminent public policy economists Ross Garnaut and Vince FitzGerald in 2002 for NSW, Victoria and Western Australia. Other states and territories dismissed it.

If we were starting with a blank sheet, EPC or some variant of it may well look like the best way to go — but the starting point consists of smaller states and territories strongly wedded to the status quo. The NT with five times its population share of GST revenue, Tasmania with almost double and South Australia with 1.4 times, will always fight tooth and nail to keep what they have, and no federal government will over-ride their objections to change.

As Peter Costello often said, if the states and territories could agree on a different method of distribution, the Commonwealth would implement it — knowing full well there would never be such agreement. The status quo has always won.

The smallest two states and the NT would lose more than $7 billion a year from a shift to EPC. Minns breezily assigns the burden of compensation to the Commonwealth. That won't happen. It would permanently lumber the federal budget with a burden even greater than the sweet deal WA extracted from the Turnbull government in 2018; to put a floor under its GST share regardless of the state's iron ore royalty windfall.

Minns and Mookhey should carry on the NSW tradition of advocating fundamental HFE reform and construct as broad a coalition of the willing as they can. They are now at loggerheads with Victoria over this year's allocations, but reform is in Victoria's longer-term interests. WA has supported reform in the past but is now happy with its top-up deal with the Commonwealth, as long as it lasts. Queensland has always been a strong defender of the status quo, but that could change down the track.

Reform is a long game. The immediate focus must be on the forthcoming budget. If Minns wants to portray the CGC report as a crisis for NSW, then he should take it as an opportunity to frame a tighter budget than otherwise. As the saying goes, never let a good crisis go to waste.

This opinion piece was originally published in 2024 by the *Australian Financial Review.*

Section Six: Housing Affordability

Robert Carling

This chapter provides a meticulous and powerful examination of the Australian housing crisis, fundamentally arguing that the persistent problem of reduced affordability is not the result of runaway demand, but rather a direct consequence of government-imposed supply restrictions. The analysis begins by systematically challenging numerous popular myths about the causes of high house prices, debunking the notions that lower global interest rates, speculative bubbles, or even the tax treatment of investors, such as negative gearing, are the primary drivers of long-term unaffordability. Instead, the papers consistently demonstrate that price appreciation is an economic inevitability when demand outstrips the supply constrained by rigid planning and zoning laws.

A major theme developed throughout the chapter is the devastating financial impact of these rules, which create an artificial scarcity of building permissions, resulting in a 'zoning effect' that adds hundreds of thousands of dollars to the cost of a dwelling, particularly in major capital cities. Furthermore, the collection critiques the political preference for demand-side subsidies, such as First Home Owners Grants, arguing that these measures merely inflate prices without delivering any structural improvement in the market, thus enriching existing owners at the taxpayer's expense. The discussion also scrutinises specific regulatory hurdles, such as the extensive and often irrational application of heritage protection, which has been allowed to expand to such a degree that it effectively cuts down new development and severely restricts the potential housing supply in high-demand inner-city areas.

To achieve genuine reform, the chapter outlines a clear set of policy recommendations, which centre on freeing up land supply, urgently reforming restrictive planning and zoning systems, and reducing inefficient transaction taxes like stamp duty. It also cautiously explores innovative policies, such as allowing individuals to use their superannuation as security for home loans, but stresses that such a measure must be strictly coupled with supply-side reforms to prevent it from exacerbating price inflation. In essence, the entire chapter serves as an unyielding call for policymakers to abandon politically safe measures and address the structural inefficiency of the housing market by removing the barriers that prevent the appropriate flow of new homes.

Eight Housing Affordability Myths

Stephen Kirchner (2014)

Executive Summary

Australia has seen strong real house price growth, reducing affordability. Governments have responded with inconsistent policies, taxing and subsidising housing simultaneously. Measures such as first home buyer grants raise demand but fail to address regulatory barriers that restrict supply. The paper argues that long-term real house price appreciation is consistent with economic fundamentals and that reform should focus on freeing up land supply, reducing transaction taxes such as stamp duty and capital gains tax, and simplifying planning processes.

Introduction

Australia's rising house prices have created a divide between owners who gain wealth and non-owners facing reduced purchasing power. Public policy has been confused — taxing and subsidising housing at multiple levels without clear benchmarks for assessing the effects. The main issue lies in supply failing to keep up with demand, as governments pursue policies that inflate demand while ignoring supply constraints.

Myth 1: Lower Interest Rates Make Housing More Affordable

Housing affordability is complex and cannot be captured by simple ratios of prices to income. While lower real interest rates have boosted borrowing capacity and asset prices, they do not make housing more affordable in the long term. Real rates are largely determined globally, not by domestic monetary policy, and their fall has led to permanent, not temporary, increases in house prices.

Myth 2: House Prices Are a Speculative 'Bubble'

There is little empirical support for claims of a speculative housing bubble. Australian house prices have tracked fundamentals such as income, population, and lower real interest rates. Short-term fluctuations are part of normal cycles. Policies aimed at suppressing demand or "bursting bubbles" — such as tighter lending rules — cannot improve long-term affordability, which depends on supply-side flexibility.

Myth 3: The Supply of Land Is Fixed

Land supply is constrained by government policy, not by physical limits. State and local planning rules have sharply reduced new land production and raised land prices. Between 2003 and the early 2010s, average lot numbers in major cities fell by 21%, while land prices rose by 148%. Expanding land release and increasing density through zoning reform are essential to improve affordability.

Myth 4: Housing Is an Unproductive Asset

Housing is productive because it provides valuable shelter and investment returns. Rents and imputed yields demonstrate its contribution to the economy. The notion that housing is unproductive arises from policy-created land scarcities, not from the nature of housing itself. Such misperceptions justify punitive taxes and discourage new supply.

Myth 5: Australians Invest Too Much in Housing

Claims that Australians over-invest in housing ignore the reality that supply has not kept pace with demand. New housing approvals have lagged behind population growth — with one new dwelling approved for every 2.73 new residents in 2013. To restore balance, more investment in housing is needed to meet demographic and lifestyle changes, including the demolition of older homes and the desire for higher quality dwellings.

Myth 6: Foreign Investors Are Responsible for Rising House Prices

Foreign investors account for only 2–3% of housing demand and are already restricted from buying existing dwellings. Blaming them for high prices distracts from domestic supply issues. Limiting foreign investment undermines housing construction finance and deters capital inflows. When foreigners buy Australian property, they transfer wealth to locals — through both new housing and higher values for existing stock.

Myth 7: Domestic Investors, Negative Gearing, and Capital Gains Tax Concessions Are Responsible for Rising House Prices

Tax rules for housing investment are consistent with those for other assets. Negative gearing and capital gains concessions make property investment more attractive, which supports both demand and supply. Curtailing these incentives without addressing supply-side constraints risks reducing rental availability and worsening affordability. Housing is already heavily taxed through GST, stamp duty, and regulatory costs — estimated to comprise up to 44% of Sydney's new home prices.

Myth 8: House Prices Are Fuelled by a Credit 'Bubble' or Excessive Leverage

Financial deregulation since the 1980s allowed households to borrow more efficiently. Rising debt levels reflect long-term structural changes, not a credit bubble. Household debt relative to income has stabilised, and mortgage arrears remain low. Increases in leverage have been matched by strong fundamentals and are unlikely to reverse substantially.

Conclusion

Australia's housing affordability problem stems from government-imposed constraints on supply rather than excessive demand. Public policy should focus on:

- Lowering taxes on housing transactions;
- Reforming zoning, planning, and approval systems;

- Avoiding demand-side subsidies such as first home grants; and
- Ensuring a steady flow of new housing.

The paper concludes that affordability will only improve when governments remove the barriers that prevent the housing market from responding to demand.

This is an edited extract of a 2014 Centre for Independent Studies research paper. The full paper can be found at https://www.cis.org.au/publication/eight-housing-affordability-myths/

Housing Affordability and Supply Restrictions

Dr Peter Tulip (2024)

Introduction

Australia has some of the most unaffordable housing in the world, with Sydney and Melbourne ranked third and fourth least affordable globally. Rising housing costs have contributed to inequality, longer commutes, rental stress and declining home ownership. Numerous government and academic reports attribute these high prices to restrictive land use policies that limit where and how much housing can be built. Most Australian cities are zoned for low-density detached housing, and where higher density is allowed, limits on building height and floor area restrict development. These planning rules create a shortage of dwellings by constraining supply, thereby pushing up prices.

This paper summarises research showing that planning restrictions substantially raise housing prices. It reviews alternative explanations, compares results with other studies, weighs the costs and benefits of restrictions, and considers whether more housing supply would make homes more affordable.

The Impact of Planning Restrictions on Housing Prices

The effect of planning restrictions can be measured by the price people pay for development approval — the legal permission to build an extra dwelling. This permission is valuable because approvals are scarce. Rezoning that allows higher density often adds hundreds of thousands of dollars to the value of a site, showing how much the right to build is worth.

In Sydney in 2016, the average house price was $1.16 million, of which only a third reflected the cost of the structure; two-thirds represented land value. However, most of that land value came not from its physical attributes but from its legal use rights. The "zoning effect" added about $489,000 — or 73% — to the cost of a Sydney house. Comparable effects were found in Melbourne (69%), Brisbane (42%) and Perth (54%).

For apartments, restrictions increased Sydney prices by 68% above supply cost, by 20% in Melbourne and 2% in Brisbane. These results imply that allowing more dense development, particularly apartments, would significantly improve affordability.

Alternative Explanations

Other studies highlight factors such as immigration, low interest rates, taxation and financialisation as drivers of housing demand. However, these factors only raise prices if supply is constrained. Without planning restrictions, rising demand would lead to more construction rather than higher prices. Hence, demand and supply explanations are complementary.

The argument also applies to location differences. For example, apartment prices in inner Sydney far exceed construction costs because new supply there is limited, while central Melbourne and Brisbane — where building has been allowed — show much smaller price premiums.

Consistency with Other Research

International research supports the conclusion that planning restrictions raise prices. Studies in the United States, New Zealand, Britain and Europe find similar or even larger effects. The methodology comparing prices with construction costs is widely accepted among economists and has been rigorously tested.

Alternative approaches, such as analysing variations in local regulations or measuring cumulative supply shortfalls, produce consistent results. The NSW Productivity Commission estimated an undersupply of 70,000 dwellings in 2019, projected to grow to 170,000 by 2038.

Costs versus Benefits of Planning Restrictions

Costs of Planning Restrictions

The main cost of planning restrictions is reduced affordability. They transfer unearned capital gains to landowners while burdening renters and first home buyers, worsening inequality. By driving a wedge between price and cost, restrictions make the housing market inefficient—people pay more but get less of what they value, such as location and space. They also restrict mobility, prevent workers from accessing high-productivity jobs and lengthen commutes.

Benefits of Planning Restrictions

Planning restrictions can preserve neighbourhood character, limit congestion and maintain aesthetic or environmental quality. Many residents prefer low-density areas. However, high-density development also offers benefits that are valued by buyers—walkable communities, proximity to shops and transport, and lower commuting times. Studies from the UK and US find little evidence that high-rises depress nearby property values. High density also brings wider social benefits, including reduced car use, lower emissions, and increased innovation and productivity. The balance of evidence suggests that the costs of restrictions exceed their benefits.

Would More Supply Make Housing More Affordable?

Evidence strongly supports the view that increasing housing supply would reduce prices. Countries such as Japan, which build housing rapidly, have lower costs, while restrictive countries like Australia face persistent affordability problems. Within the US, cities with flexible building rules, such as Atlanta and Houston, are far more affordable than highly regulated ones like San Francisco or New York.

Although some argue that additional supply would only marginally affect prices, research shows that a 1% increase in housing stock can reduce prices by about 2.5%. Doubling annual housing construction could therefore lower prices by around 5% per year, although reversing decades of under-building would take time.

Claims that new apartment supply is already adequate are misplaced: growth rates may be high, but the absolute level of housing remains below what is needed. Even after temporary downturns, prices remain well above construction costs, showing an enduring shortage.

Conclusion

Planning restrictions are a major cause of high housing prices in Australia. They reduce affordability, entrench inequality and restrict economic efficiency. While residents' preferences for low density and aesthetic considerations are valid, the evidence shows that the costs of current planning rules greatly outweigh their benefits. Allowing more building — especially in high-demand inner-city areas — would make housing more affordable, stimulate productivity and improve social welfare.

> This is an edited extract of a 2024 Centre for Independent Studies research paper. The full paper can be found at https://www.cis.org.au/publication/housing-affordability-and-supply-restrictions/

Super for Housing

Matthew Taylor and Dr Peter Tulip (2025)

Introduction

This research report explored the potential benefits and challenges of allowing Australians to access their superannuation to purchase a home. The proposal aims to increase homeownership, provide more flexibility in retirement savings, and address housing affordability issues. However, it also raises concerns about reduced retirement incomes and potential increases in housing prices. The report evaluates these issues and proposes solutions to mitigate the downsides.

Rationale for using super to help buy housing

Superannuation and home equity are both ways to save for retirement. Allowing individuals to use super for housing gives them more choice in how they prepare for retirement. Using super for housing could be a more efficient and equitable way to promote homeownership than existing policies like First Home Owners Grants. Many first-home buyers face deposit constraints. Accessing super could help overcome these barriers, reducing the need for costly financial intermediation (e.g., simultaneously saving and borrowing).

Benefits of using super for housing

The median first-home buyer could increase their deposit by 92% if allowed to access their super. This could either enable them to buy a home sooner or purchase a more suitable property.

Allowing super for housing could bring forward home purchases by an average of 2.8 years, potentially increasing homeownership rates by 4 percentage points (from 66% to 70%). Replacing First Home Owners Grants with super for housing could provide more assistance to buyers at a lower fiscal cost, while reducing distortions in the housing market.

Concerns and mitigations

Withdrawing super for housing could reduce retirement savings. For example, a typical borrower who withdraws $62,500 and repays it after 10 years could have $53,600 less in their retirement account at age 65. This could be avoided by using super as collateral for home loans instead of withdrawing funds. Increased demand for housing could drive up prices, exacerbating affordability issues. To address this, the policy should be coupled with measures to increase housing supply, such as relaxing planning restrictions. Homeownership is already heavily subsidised, favouring wealthier individuals. Super for housing could exacerbate this inequity unless it replaces less equitable subsidies like First Home Owners Grants.

Quantitative estimates

The median deposit paid by first-home buyers in the three years up to 2019-20 was $68,200 while the median super balance of first-home buyers was $62,500. This suggests that accessing super could allow first-home buyers to increase their deposit by 92% or reduce the cash they had to save for a deposit by 92%.

Allowing super for housing could enable 392,000 households to buy a home earlier, increasing the home-ownership rate by 4 percentage points. Evidence from New Zealand's KiwiSaver scheme suggests that 84% of first-home buyers would likely access their super for housing if given the opportunity.

Alternative policy approaches

Borrowers could withdraw super funds and repay them later, including a share of capital gains. This approach reduces retirement savings but increases home equity. Super could be used as security for home loans, reducing the need for large deposits without depleting retirement savings.

This approach avoids reducing super balances unless a foreclosure occurs, which is rare. Super for housing could replace less efficient subsidies like First Home Owners Grants, providing more assistance to buyers at a lower fiscal cost.

Secondary effects

Buyers might use super to purchase larger or better located homes, buy earlier, or reduce their mortgage. The policy change could also encourage some renters to become homeowners. Many first-home buyers receive financial help from parents. Super for housing could complement or reduce the need for such assistance.

Recommendations

To avoid reducing retirement savings, super should be used as security for home loans rather than allowing withdrawals. To prevent housing price inflation, super for housing should be paired with policies to increase housing supply, such as relaxing zoning restrictions. Super for housing should replace less effective policies like First Home Owners Grants, which are costly and inequitable. Policymakers should closely monitor how buyers use super for housing to ensure the policy achieves its goals without unintended consequences.

Conclusion

Allowing Australians to access their super for housing could significantly increase homeownership rates and provide more flexibility in retirement planning. However, careful design is needed to avoid reducing retirement incomes and exacerbating housing affordability issues. By using super as collateral and coupling the policy with measures to increase housing supply, the government can promote homeownership while safeguarding retirement savings.

This is an edited extract of a 2025 Centre for Independent Studies research paper. The full paper can be found at https://www.cis.org.au/publication/super-for-housing/

Negative gearing barely affects the price of houses in the market

Robert Carling (2024)

As a rule, if you tax something more you will end up with less of it. This is a well-worn epithet of tax policy debate, but generally true. In the current context, the 'something' is housing — and specifically housing held by investors.

The prospect of ending up with less of it should focus the minds of the Prime Minister and the Treasurer as they reportedly contemplate tax increases (in the form of changes to negative gearing and capital gains tax rules) to satisfy the Greens' price for supporting the Help to Buy shared housing equity scheme. Just what they are contemplating and how serious they are about it are unknowns, but the now familiar word games being played in Canberra are an ominous sign.

The Prime Minister says of changing negative gearing rules "I have no plans to do it. It is not our policy"; but Treasury just happens to be examining options for change … which may or may not have been requested by the government.

If you think you've heard this humbug before, you are right. It was the formula used early this year to wriggle out of the Stage 3 income tax cuts as structured by the previous government, and in March 2023 to launch the new tax on superannuation balances above $3 million.

A pattern is emerging. The Albanese government takes or creates opportunities to make tax changes it always wanted to make but did not dare include in its 'small target' 2022 election platform.

Ministers deny there are any plans for a change; but plans themselves can always change, and then suddenly they do. Leaving aside the grubby politics, negative gearing and capital gains tax rules need to be considered on their merits as tax policy and as housing policy.

They are first and foremost tax policies, as they apply across the board to all investments, not just housing. From a tax policy perspective, negative gearing follows the principle that the costs of generating income are a legitimate deduction. As such, it has always been part of the federal income tax, except for a two year interlude in the 1980s. The same principle applies to other investments without the objections we see in the area of housing.

Negative gearing means the investor has borrowed so much to buy a property that the mortgage interest expense is large enough, along with other running costs such as rates, to generate an annual loss. This can then be deducted from any other taxable income, including wage income, at the taxpayer's marginal rate. In 2020/21, about half of all individual property investors were in this situation — and with higher interest rates, probably a larger proportion now.

Negative gearing is a leveraged investment and as such is risky, not a one-way bet. A before-tax loss is still a loss after tax — just a smaller one. It is a losing strategy unless capital gains are sufficient to offset the operating losses over time.

While negative gearing and the 50 per cent capital gains tax discount are often mentioned in the same breath, the justification for the CGT discount (on housing as well as other assets) stands on its own. The case for negative gearing deductions is not weakened by the CGT discount, and vice versa.

However, there is a reasonable argument that negative gearing losses should not be a deduction from other regular income such as wages, but from capital gains. If the taxpayer does not have enough gains to absorb losses in a given year, they can carry the excess losses forward to deduct them from future gains.

The real objection to negative gearing often seems to be that it is allegedly directing a tax 'concession' disproportionately to well-off taxpayers. In 2020/21, more than half the tax benefit went to the top 20 per cent. However, those taxpayers pay a disproportionately large share of tax in the first place.

From a housing policy perspective, there is a view that housing affordability for owner-occupiers can be improved by discouraging investors through tax measures. While removing or reducing negative gearing and/or CGT concessions would reduce investor demand for housing, this overlooks the supply effects. The withdrawal of some investors from the market would lead to less housing being supplied, muting the fall in prices. Owner-occupier demand would not neatly fill the void left by departing investors, as the types of housing favoured by investors and owner-occupiers are not perfectly interchangeable.

While tilting the composition of the existing housing stock from rental to owner-occupied might make some people feel better, because home ownership is highly valued, it would also exacerbate tightness in the rental market.

There are several studies of the impact of negative gearing (and the CGT discount) on dwelling prices and they all find that it is very small — in the order of 1 to 4 per cent; not per year, but in total over many years. Conversely, any price relief from curbing negative gearing would be small.

So if stopping negative gearing is bad tax policy and even worse housing policy, why even contemplate doing it? One explanation is that the government will cave in to the Greens out of desperation to get Help to Buy up and running. Another is that it is secretly happy to be pushed into doing something it wanted to do anyway — slash tax breaks — and blame the Greens. It is probably a bit of both.

This opinion piece was originally published in 2024 by *The Australian.*

How heritage protection is cutting down housing development

Simon Cowan and Dr Peter Tulip (2023)

More and more people are realising the only meaningful solution to our housing affordability crisis is to unlock the barriers that prevent housing being built. There is growing appreciation that the traditional approach of subsidising demand doesn't work. The lucky recipients bid up prices, making housing more expensive for everyone else. Unless supply increases, demand-side measures just reshuffle a fixed housing stock — at substantial cost to the taxpayer. Unfortunately, these lessons are yet to be learnt by the Queensland government, which last week doubled grants to First Home Buyers; or the Commonwealth, which just increased subsidies to risky borrowers (undoing the efforts of APRA to prevent that very borrowing).

Housing supply advocates are starting behind in many areas. The anti-development crowd have had decades to erect barricades, and each requires concerted effort to tear them down. One such barrier is heritage protection. Heritage protection sounds like a good idea in theory. many people admire and want to preserve the old and attractive features of our cities and towns. But it has been allowed to run amok.

It is important to understand that heritage protection is not just extended to historically significant things but also to items of alleged scientific, cultural, social, archaeological, architectural, natural or aesthetic curiosity. This has meant that heritage has extended to items whose significance or appeal is very narrow. Indeed, many of the buildings being listed have no appeal to the broader public. Some are widely regarded as eyesores.

When the McKinnon Foundation polled Australians about their concerns with increased housing density, only 10 per cent of respondents mentioned heritage in their top 5. "Losing built heritage" came in 17th out of 18 possible concerns. Yet heritage protection has exploded across many suburbs. The City of Sydney now has over 50% of its land under Heritage Conservation Areas or heritage items, while Sydney's inner west council has more than 40%.

Vast swathes of territory have been turned into little more than living museums, including most of Haberfield, Balmain, Glebe, Hunters Hill, Woolwich, and much of the north shore on the east side of the Pacific Highway. Unsurprisingly, admission to these museums is now often $3-4 million or more. The problem is that heritage protection — which should serve as a shield to protect a rather limited sweep of items of genuine historical significance — has become a sword wielded to cut down new development. And in the hands of those who wish to see nothing change in 'their' suburb, it has held development hostage to an increasingly absurd and irrational list of demands.

For example, in April the City of Melbourne listed a 1970s seven-storey concrete carpark. In June, Sydney's Inner West Council proposed listing 15 electricity substations. The NSW Heritage Council has opposed the construction of high-rise buildings at Central Station in Sydney, suggesting that low density would be more appropriate for that location.

With our housing affordability crisis escalating, we cannot allow a tiny minority to encase the country in a stasis cube. Heritage protection has been able to expand largely unnoticed because its costs are hidden. But it is not costless. Not only does heritage often directly prevent the building of new, denser, housing (which is an obvious cost), it imposes unwieldy restrictions on the use of existing housing. Those who own heritage-listed properties are frustrated seemingly at every turn when seeking to make their properties more liveable.

One way to assess the true cost of heritage protection is to compare the value of a property under its restricted heritage use with the potential value of that property if it was unencumbered. For an inner-city block of land that otherwise might support a medium-rise apartment building, that cost will be many millions of dollars. Then imagine multiplying that across the number of properties in all the suburbs identified above. That is the true cost of the heritage regime. This suggests one simple way to get people to understand the scale of the problem would be to task the Productivity Commission with an estimate of the current cost of heritage protection in Australia; together with recommendations on how to lower this cost.

Going forward, councils and heritage bodies should be required to include an estimate of the true cost of all new heritage listings, together with a justification for who should bear that cost. This would also make clear the unbelievably disproportionate emphasis placed on protecting historical architecture compared to the rest of our history. NSW spends about $360 million a year on operating costs for artistic and cultural institutions, like the Art Gallery of NSW and the Australian Museum. That may not even cover the cost of heritage protection in a single Sydney suburb.

We should fundamentally change the nature of heritage protection, whilst ensuring that truly important historical buildings are preserved but also valued. Instead of endless regulation, governments (federal, state and local) could be required to purchase historically significant buildings they wish to preserve and make them open to the public to admire and visit.

This will make clear if the buildings or items really are significant to the general public, both because the cost to taxpayers will be transparent and people will actually come to see them — or not, in many cases. For example, it is hard to imagine that many people would choose to visit a concrete car park where you couldn't park your car.

But perhaps more importantly, it will make clear whether the public truly values heritage to the level that is implied by the current protections, or if heritage protection is just another NIMBY racket.

This opinion piece was originally published in 2023 by the *Canberra Times*.

Section Seven: Superannuation

Robert Carling

This chapter offers a profound critique of the prevailing architecture of Australian retirement income policy, focusing its analysis on two key components: the compulsory superannuation system and the findings of the 2021 Retirement Income Review. The initial papers contend that after what was then two decades, the compulsory superannuation system has fundamentally failed to achieve its core objectives, particularly in its original aim to significantly boost national saving. Instead, the scheme is described as a poor example of paternalism which imposes considerable deadweight costs and administrative burdens, effectively functioning as an involuntary retirement tax that disproportionately affects low-income earners by substituting forced saving for the voluntary accumulation of wealth.

Another section discusses the vexed issue of the appropriate structure and level of taxation of superannuation, which has been a constant theme of public policy debate and action almost ever since the Howard government's 'simpler super' reforms of 2006. It is argued that while different structures of superannuation tax might well be superior to what we have, the opportunity for that has long passed and in that context the 'simpler super' structure is the next best and that much of the tinkering of the last 15 years or so is unwarranted on grounds of efficiency and equity and has added a great deal to complexity and to compliance costs.

Moving to the broader policy framework, a later section of the chapter takes serious issue with the implicit preferences of the 2001 Retirement Income Review, suggesting that its standards for retirement adequacy and its focus on discouraging people from dying with residual wealth amount to a public encouragement of private profligacy. The collection warns that, given the precarious state of public finances and the deteriorating trade environment, policies that actively discourage long-term private saving and thrift are fundamentally unwise. The overriding argument of the entire chapter is that long-term retirement policy requires fundamental structural reform, prioritising individual choice and a return to the virtues of thrift and personal responsibility, rather than maintaining complex, costly, and ultimately ineffective government mandates.

Compulsory Super at 20: Libertarian Paternalism without the Libertarianism

Stephen Kirchner (2012)

Executive Summary

The Australian compulsory superannuation system (Super Guarantee) is often presented as a solution to under-saving for retirement, addressing potential 'market failures' through 'libertarian paternalism' (a nudge towards saving). However, after 20 years, the system has failed to meet its original objectives.

- Superannuation has not significantly increased national saving; it has merely changed the composition of saving, substituting compulsory super saving for voluntary saving.
- The system has had little measurable impact on population ageing, as the increase in national saving required to offset demographic change would be far larger than that delivered by superannuation.
- Compulsory super has imposed significant deadweight costs and administrative burdens, including high fees and charges, that disproportionately affect low-income earners, effectively acting as an 'involuntary retirement tax'.
- The system is an example of paternalism without libertarianism, as it forces participation with little opportunity for individuals to opt out or exercise genuine choice.

The paper recommends a phased abolition of compulsory superannuation or, failing that, reforms to reduce its complexity, including: making contributions voluntary above a threshold, lowering fees, and increasing flexibility for early access to contributions.

Defining and measuring household and national saving

Saving is the difference between income and consumption. The paper stresses the distinction between household saving (the net change in household wealth) and national saving (saving by all sectors of the economy). While the SG forces an increase in household saving, it may be offset by an increase in consumption or a decrease in saving in other forms (e.g., increased debt).

Does Australia have a national saving problem?

Australia's national saving rate has fallen since the 1970s, but this is a global trend reflecting a slowdown in private capital accumulation. National saving is not an end in itself; it should be measured against the 'Golden Rule' benchmark which suggests Australia is either at or above its optimal long-run saving rate. Furthermore, the argument that Australia suffers from persistently low household saving is flawed, as Australia's saving rate is comparable to the OECD average and is likely understated by official statistics.

National saving and population ageing.

The primary justification for compulsory super is to help fund the future costs of an ageing population. However, the required increase in national saving to offset demographic change would be seven to ten percentage points of GDP over 25 years. The SG has delivered, at most, a two-percentage-point increase in national saving, making its impact on this problem negligible. Moreover, the SG is unlikely to fully substitute the Age Pension due to the low accumulated balances of many low-income and part-time workers.

Compulsory super, the labour market, and household saving

The SG has had a negative impact on the labour market and household saving behaviour:

- Labour Market: The SG is effectively a tax on labour, as compulsory contributions are likely borne by employees through lower wages rather than by employers. This reduces the employment of low-wage workers and imposes an efficiency cost (deadweight loss).
- **Household Saving:** The SG is a weak form of compulsory saving as it does not enforce a minimum total household saving rate. Evidence suggests the SG has simply substituted compulsory saving for voluntary saving (known as the 'Ricardian equivalence effect'), resulting in little net increase in total household saving.

Saving adequately for retirement: Market failure or government failure?

The argument for compulsory super rests on the idea of 'market failure' (e.g., individuals being short-sighted or lacking financial literacy). However, the evidence suggests the SG itself has led to 'government failure':

- **High Costs:** The SG involves high fees and charges (estimated at $19 billion in 2011–12), which disproportionately reduce the returns for low-income earners.
- **Complexity:** The system is overly complex, leading to compliance costs and an inefficient allocation of capital.
- **Unintended Consequences:** The tax concessions for superannuation predominantly benefit high-income earners, failing to achieve the objective of providing a retirement income safety net.

Conclusion and recommendations

Compulsory super is an inefficient policy that has failed to deliver a measurable increase in national saving while imposing a large, regressive 'involuntary retirement tax' on low-income earners.

Recommendations

1. **Abolish the Super Guarantee (SG):** The most effective reform is the phased elimination of the SG, to be replaced by a voluntary, tax-preferred saving system.

2. **Voluntary Contributions:** Alternatively, make contributions above an initial low threshold (e.g., 3%) voluntary.

3. **Reduce Costs:** Implement measures to dramatically reduce the fees and charges on superannuation accounts.

4. **Increase Flexibility:** Allow early access to a portion of compulsory contributions (e.g., for major expenses like a first home).

This is an edited extract of a 2012 Centre for Independent Studies research paper. The full paper can be found at https://www.cis.org.au/publication/compulsory-super-at-20-libertarian-paternalism-without-the-libertarianism/

Millennials and Super: the case for voluntary superannuation

Simon Cowan (2019)

Superannuation is a compulsory retirement savings scheme with well known problems, including high fees and low returns, and it is failing to deliver independence from the Age Pension. Although a tax-advantaged long-term savings vehicle should exist , the system has been constantly reformed without resolving its fundamental issues. This report questions whether the workforce should be compelled to remain in the superannuation system and explores the negative impact that compulsory super may be having on homeownership rates, especially for millennials.

Retirement income priorities

Australia's retirement system rests on three pillars: the Age Pension, compulsory super, and other savings. However, the single biggest factor determining a comfortable retirement is homeownership. Homeowners receiving the full Age Pension have approximately nine times the net worth of non-homeowners on the same income. This suggests that prioritising homeownership over increasing superannuation balances is a logical decision that should not be legally prevented. The compulsory system is a form of paternalism, which relies on the assumptions that individuals systemically under-save, this causes serious harm (old age poverty), and their consumption patterns are irrational. However, the Age Pension is likely sufficient to address old age poverty.

Housing affordability and its potential impact on retirement

The declining rate of homeownership among millennials is a major concern. Since compulsory super was introduced, the ratio of house prices to incomes has worsened. While low interest rates have reduced mortgage servicing costs, they have not offset the difficulty of raising a deposit, with the average deposit as a multiple of average earnings almost doubling between 2000 and 2015. Compulsory super, which docks nearly 10% of income (set to rise to 12% in 2025), is a hindrance to lower-middle income earners saving for a deposit, meaning the system prioritises superannuation above homeownership. Homeownership rates have fallen across all age groups since 1991, with the biggest falls among the 25-34 and 35-44 age groups.

A 1980s industrial model of super doesn't fit changing work patterns

The highly regulated and rigid superannuation system is poorly suited to the increasingly flexible nature of work. The system is rooted in a rigid industrial relations system. The modern trend of increased part-time work across the board means that working part-time for long periods, even at a median wage, results in a substantial reduction in the final super balance. Career breaks and part-time work significantly reduce savings, and while this disproportionately affects women/mothers, the underlying problem is the rigidity of the system against modern work patterns.

Do savings patterns match superannuation?

The compulsory system diverts resources away from the more important priorities of buying a home and raising a family. Furthermore, individuals' savings rates rarely match those mandated by legislation, indicating they are actively using workarounds to create their own necessary savings flexibility. These workarounds (e.g., taking on personal loans or credit card debt to be paid off with future super) are inefficient and represent an unappreciated cost of compulsory saving.

Mortgage debt and its impact on superannuation

There has been a significant increase in the amount of mortgage debt held by those moving into retirement. The biggest increases in the percentage of homeowners with a mortgage have been in the 55-64, 45-54, and 35-44 age groups. This means the compulsory system is increasingly forcing workers to save for mortgage repayment rather than solely for retirement income.

Conclusion

Compulsory superannuation is not a good deal for everyone. The system needs to be rethought due to three key issues: the hindrance it poses to saving for a home deposit, its poor fit with flexible work patterns, and the need for greater flexibility in savings choices. A voluntary system, or one with a much higher threshold for compulsory participation, would be a welcome improvement.

This is an edited extract of a 2019 Centre for Independent Studies research paper. The full paper can be found at https://www.cis.org.au/publication/millennials-and-super-the-case-for-voluntary-superannuation/

How Should Super be Taxed?

Robert Carling (2016)

The Turnbull government's proposed changes to superannuation taxes and rules, announced in the May 2016 budget, were a reaction to claims of excessive generosity in the 2007 reforms. Critics primarily claimed that no tax applied to fund earnings or member withdrawals after age 60, the system lacked 'progressivity' due to flat taxes, and members could accumulate too much capital. The government's far-reaching changes aimed to address these criticisms.

The budget imperative

Moves to restrict superannuation and raise revenue occurred due to a persistent budget deficit. The author argues that the budget problem primarily stems from excess expenditure rather than deficient revenue. The government's 2016 budget proposed a revenue-neutral package, aiming for a small net increase from superannuation (forecast at $1.1 billion a year by 2019-2020) offset by tax reductions elsewhere. The commonly cited figure of $30 billion a year for a revenue shortfall or 'tax expenditure' is dismissed as invalid because it uses an inappropriate tax structure benchmark.

How should saving be taxed?

Superannuation is a form of saving, and the default income tax treatment of saving creates a strong bias against it, particularly long-term saving. Concessional taxation of long-term savings, such as superannuation and owner-occupied housing, is considered a 'correction to avoid artificially crippling long-term saving'. The current system's structure is similar to a simple bank deposit, meaning there is no inherent need for a tax at the third (pension) phase for the overall tax take to be correct. However, the Coalition's proposal to cap the pension balance eligible for tax-exempt earnings (at $1.6 million) effectively acts as a third-stage tax by reducing the fund's capacity to pay a pension. The author argues that any restriction on the principle of zero taxation in the third stage based on pension fund size is arbitrary and risks future arbitrary tightening.

Equity

Perceptions of a lack of 'progressivity' are a major driver of the proposed changes, as higher income earners appear to benefit disproportionately from tax concessions. The changes aim to steepen the progressivity in contributions tax and introduce a new progressive element to fund earnings tax. The author counters that 'fairness' must consider the tax/transfer system as a whole and a lifetime view. The Australian system relies on the progressive personal income tax structure and means testing of income support to deliver distributional fairness. Although superannuation concessions are skewed towards higher income deciles, the personal income tax burden is even more skewed, with the richest 20% paying a greater share of income tax than they receive in concessions. When the Age Pension payments (currently $45 billion a year) and the lifetime dimension are included, the distribution of benefits is much smoother.

Access limits

Limits on contributions are needed to manage revenue consequences because superannuation is taxed more lightly than other savings. The tightening of limits in the 2016 budget is described as draconian, with insufficient reasoned justification. Key changes include:

- A reduction in non-concessional contributions from $540,000 over three years to $500,000 over a lifetime.
- The introduction of a $1.6 million balance cap on a retirement fund free of the 15% earnings tax. These limits are criticised for lacking an actuarial basis and flexibility. It is contested that $1.6 million is

sufficient to fund a pension four times the public age pension, with some estimates suggesting $3.2 million is needed. The lifetime limit on non-concessional contributions is considered far too low, given these contributions are made from after-tax income.

Simplicity

Simplicity was a goal of the 2007 changes, which streamlined the system and removed tax on payouts over age 60. The proposed changes risk adding complexity. The proposed $1.6 million cap on pension funds will impose a new compliance burden on fund administrators, requiring the aggregation of multiple accounts and the actuarial conversion of defined benefit pensions. Similarly, the proposed lifetime cap on non-concessional contributions will require multi-year record keeping and aggregation.

Conclusion

The superannuation tax regime's principle of concessional taxation is justified, but its degree has been eroded by past and proposed increases in contributions tax and the tightening of caps. The changes respond to budget pressures and calls for 'fairness'. The overall tax/transfer system is already highly redistributive, and flat superannuation taxes offer significant simplification benefits. While limits are needed, the tightening proposed is draconian and lacks sufficient justification, leading the author to recommend the government produce a green paper for consultation, including the actuarial basis for revised proposals.

This is an edited extract of a Centre for Independent Studies article from the Policy quarterly magazine, Spring 2016 edition.

Building a Better Super System

Simon Cowan (2016)

Executive Summary

Both major political parties presented superannuation reform packages in the lead-up to the federal election, largely addressing the concern that 'excessive' tax concessions were benefiting high-income earners. The proposals included lowering the income cap for additional tax on concessional contributions, imposing a tax on wealthy retirees, and boosting contributions for low-income earners. The Coalition's package went further by capping non-concessional contributions and scrapping the Transition to Retirement (TTR) provisions, which were found to be primarily used by full-time workers to minimise tax.

The primary focus of the policy debate was the tax revenue being lost due to these concessions. However, the true purpose of the superannuation system should be to ensure Australians can save adequately to reduce their reliance on the Age Pension, thus creating long-term savings for the government. The paper proposes that future superannuation reform should be Age Pension-centric.

Is super reducing age pension reliance?

The ability of superannuation to offset the cost of the Age Pension remains questionable. The Productivity Commission (PC) estimated that for every $1 saved in super, Age Pension costs are only reduced by 22 cents for low-income earners, with the overall reduction being around 10 cents.

- This modest reduction is due to two factors: the superannuation system having a high proportion of people who do not contribute and high-income earners who would be ineligible for the Age Pension regardless of their super savings.

- The PC found that only 56% of the population made compulsory contributions, and only 47% made contributions that would actually reduce their Age Pension entitlement.

The Age Pension savings benchmark

The core objective of superannuation reform should be to improve the efficiency of the system in achieving its central, stated aim: to reduce the long-term cost of the Age Pension.

- Future policy changes should be measured against an Age Pension Savings (APS) benchmark—the total reduction in future Age Pension expenditure created by any proposal.
- Tax concessions should be focused on the cohort of people (estimated to be in the mid-to-high income range) who are most likely to increase their superannuation savings enough to move them off or onto a lower rate of the Age Pension.

Policy recommendations

The paper suggests two key reforms to improve the efficiency of superannuation as an Age Pension substitute:

1. Reduce the income threshold for the concessional contributions tax: Lowering the Division 293 tax threshold (which imposes an additional 15% tax on contributions) will reduce the benefits for high-income earners who are unlikely to ever receive the Age Pension, thereby directing tax concessions more efficiently.
2. Abolish the Transition to Retirement (TTR) scheme: This scheme offers a major tax concession that primarily benefits high-income earners without a corresponding benefit to the Age Pension system, and its removal would free up revenue for more effective policy measures.

This is an edited extract of a Centre for Independent Studies article from the *Policy quarterly magazine*, Spring 2016 edition.

Implications of the Retirement Income Review: Public advocacy of private profligacy?

Terrence O'Brien (2021)

Introduction

The 2020 Retirement Income Review (the Review) implies policy directions that would heavily tax saving growth within the superannuation fund, apply this new, higher tax to income in the retirement phase, and encourage the more rapid spending of savings, including the equity in the family home, to minimise bequests. These policies would incline each generation towards consuming fully its own lifetime savings. The Review claims that retirement saving is more than adequate for most people — except renters — based on a standard that an adequate retirement income is 65% to 75% of average after-tax income in the last 10 years of work.

The superannuation system

Superannuation has had specific tax treatment since 1915 due to its compulsory preservation. The introduction of the Superannuation Guarantee (SG) in 1992 and the Simplified Superannuation measures of 2007 have shaped the modern system. The SG mandated saving and led to a net increase in household saving. Simplified Superannuation aimed to "improve incentives to work and save" by conditionally removing income tax on superannuation drawdowns in retirement. The value of assets in super funds has grown to about 175% of annual GDP. Age Pension expenditure reached $46 billion in 2018-19, but projections of Age and Service Pension expenditure as a share of GDP are now projected to fall significantly, and the proportion of the age-eligible population receiving any Age Pension is also projected to decline. However, the Review worries that Treasury's annually estimated 'tax expenditures' on super are very high and rising, potentially approaching the amount spent on Age and Service Pensions.

The Retirement Income Review

The Retirement Income Review was commissioned in September 2019 to establish a "fact base" of the system and its impact on public finances. Its central finding is that the retirement income system is "effective, sound and its costs are broadly sustainable". It concludes that the structure "broadly supports intergenerational equity" as superannuation saving reduces the burden of the Age Pension on the working age population.

Changing official attitudes to saving?

While thrift and homeownership were once considered a bedrock Australian value, the Review seems to have arrived at a "rather different view".

The Review implies that the role of superannuation in national saving may be disregarded and that the compulsory SG rate need not rise. It heavily implies that the 15 per cent tax rate on super fund earnings should be significantly raised — potentially to the taxpayer's marginal rate (e.g., 32.5% or 30%) — to mimic the taxation of income from a savings account outside superannuation. The current 15% rate is highlighted as driving the rising cost of claimed super 'tax expenditures'. The Review also suggests the recreation of very high effective marginal tax rates on saving by the 2017 increase in the Age Pension asset test taper doesn't matter much.

Income adequacy in retirement

Most people will have enough funds to meet the Review's judgement of "retirement income adequacy" under current policies. The Review encourages more rapid spending of saving in retirement. It is concerned that some people die with more wealth than they retired with, presenting this as a problem for retirement income policy. This concern is raised despite the family home — which is typically not held in super — representing

40% of average household wealth and often appreciating over 30 years of retirement. The Review suggests the compulsory SG contribution rate need not rise, as current savings will be adequate for most.

The Review's key retirement income 'facts'

The Review's analysis is underpinned by two key 'facts': first, that hypothesised 'tax expenditures' on superannuation are too high and rising (projected to exceed Age Pension costs) due to the low earnings tax rate ; and second, the related claim that superannuation concessions allegedly increase inequality.

The Review's central concern about high and rising 'tax expenditures' rests entirely on its choice of an unjustified hypothetical 'comprehensive income tax' benchmark. This benchmark has never been explicitly adopted by any government and is biased against saving, particularly long-term saving.

The alternative expenditure tax benchmark for tax expenditures

A reputable alternative is the expenditure tax benchmark, which is savings-neutral and would reveal 'tax expenditures' to be much lower and flatter. Factoring in the means testing of the Age Pension pushes the effective tax rate on compulsory superannuation towards 40 per cent or more. Under the alternative benchmark, the richest 10% receive less than $150,000 in lifetime 'tax expenditures' while the poorest 10% receive over $300,000 in lifetime support (mostly Age Pension).

Hoarding in retirement?

The Review is concerned about people dying with more wealth than they retired with, which is presented as a problem of retirement income policy.

The standard for adequacy used by the Review is 65% to 75% of average after-tax income in the last 10 years of work. Given the extraordinary setbacks to the fiscal and public debt situation since the COVID-19 pandemic and the deteriorating trade environment, policies that discourage long-term saving and encourage profligacy are unwise.

Conclusion

The Review's implied policy preferences amount to a public encouragement of private profligacy. Their logical endpoint is that ideally, each generation should consume its lifetime capital, leaving each new generation at a 'year zero' from which to build and in turn then consume their own capital. Seldom has any report's policy inclinations been so quickly challenged by events. Robert Menzies had wise views on the virtues of thrift, and a few words apposite to the Retirement Income

Review. He warned in 1942: "...If the motto is to be 'Eat, drink and be merry, for tomorrow you will die, and if it chances you don't die, the State will look after you; but if you don't eat, drink and be merry and save, we shall take your savings from you', then the whole business of life would become foundationless.

This is an edited extract of a 2021 Centre for Independent Studies research paper. The full paper can be found at https://www.cis.org.au/publication/implications-of-the-retirement-income-review-public-advocacy-of-private-profligacy/

Authors

Andrew Baker is Assistant Director, Retail Banking and Currency, at the Commonwealth Treasury. He was formerly a Research Fellow at The Centre for Independent Studies. Before joining the CIS, Andrew worked in a policy research and advisory capacity for several members of the Australian Senate, and left CIS to be a ministerial adviser in the Abbott and Turnbull Governments in the social services and employment portfolios. He later joined the Australian Public Service working on diverse policy areas including disability employment, housing and homelessness, social security, consumer credit, credit reporting, and banking. He has a master's degree in Public Policy and Management from the University of Melbourne and a BA (Hons) in Philosophy from Monash University.

Professor Lauchlan Chipman graduated with a Bachelor of Philosophy (Distinction) and a Doctor of Philosophy from Oxford (where he was reportedly the inspiration for his flatmate Michael Palin's later 'Bruces' skit with Monty Python.) Prof Chipman was Senior Lecturer in Philosophy at Melbourne University, Emeritus Professor of Philosophy at Bond University, Vice Chancellor and President of Central Queensland University, Foundation Professor of Philosophy and later Pro Vice Chancellor at the University of Wollongong, Deputy Vice Chancellor at Monash University, and Vice Chancellor and President of Central Queensland University. He was also Liberal Arts Fellow in Law and Philosophy at Harvard University Law School and a Fellow of the Australian College of Education. Professor Chipman was also pivotal in the early days of The Centre for Independent Studies, delivering a paper at its inaugural seminar in 1976 and going on to serve as an academic advisor.

Simon Cowan was formerly Research Director at the CIS. He is a leading commentator on policy and politics, with a regular column in the Canberra Times newspaper, frequent interviews on Sky and the ABC, and multiple appearances before parliamentary committees discussing the budget, citizenship, taxation and health policy. He has written extensively on government spending and fiscal policy, with a specific focus on welfare and superannuation policy. He earlier work focused on government industry policy, defence and regulation.

Jim Cox was Deputy Chair of the Australian Energy Regulator from June 2020 to June 2024 and a board member from 2013 to 2024. Jim has held positions with the Reserve Bank of Australia, the Department of Prime Minister and Cabinet and the Social Policy Secretariat of the Department of Social Security. He was a principal economist at Economic Planning Advisory Commission between 1986-89 and principal adviser to the Government Pricing Tribunal from 1992 and a member of the Independent Pricing Tribunal of NSW from 1996 to 2013. Between 2004 and 2013, he was also chief executive of the Independent Pricing and Regulatory Tribunal. Jim was awarded the Public Service medal in the Australia Day honours list in 2011 for outstanding public service.

Dr Oliver Hartwich is the Executive Director of The New Zealand Initiative. He worked at the CIS as a Research Fellow in Economics and prior to working at the CIS, Oliver was the Chief Economist at the British think tank, Policy Exchange, London. Oliver's area of expertise is local government and federalism, urban economics, European affairs and Industry policy. He studied Business Administration and Economics at Bochum University (Germany). After graduating with a Master's Degree, he completed a PhD in Law at the universities of Bochum and Sydney (Australia) while working as a Researcher at the Institute of Commercial Law of Bonn University (Germany).

Dr John Humphreys is Chief Economist at the Australian Taxpayers Alliance. He was formerly an Associate Researcher at the Centre for Independent Studies, and has previously worked as a policy analyst with the Australian Treasury, lecturer at the University of Queensland and University of Sunshine Coast, and as a consultant for the Centre for

International Economics. He graduated with a Bachelor of Economics from Queensland University and completed a PhD in Economics there.

Dr Steven Kates is an Adjunct Associate Professor at RMIT University, and was formerly the Chief Economist for the Australian Chamber of Commerce and Industry. He is the author of *Free Market Economics: An Introduction for the General Reader* (Edward Elgar – third edition 2017) which is a restatement for the twenty-first century of John Stuart Mill's 1848 Principles of Political Economy. In his text, he explains what economic theory looks like if the supply-side of the economy is placed at the centre of economic analysis and in which Say's Law is brought back as the core principle underlying macro theory.

Dr Stephen Kirchner is Deputy Chief Economist at the Business Council of Australia. Previously, he was Program Director, International Economy at the United States Studies Centre, University of Sydney; Director of Economics at the Australian Financial Markets Association; Senior Lecturer in Economic at UTS Business School, University of Technology Sydney; and a Research Fellow at the CIS. Stephen has a PhD in economics from the University of New South Wales. He now writes at https://stephenkirchner.substack.com/.

Professor Tony Makin was Professor of Economics at Griffith University and previously taught at the University of Queensland, the Lee Kuan Yew School of Public Policy at the National University of Singapore, and in the Australia and New Zealand School of Government (ANZSOG) program. His field of expertise was international macroeconomics and public finance and he previously served as an economist with the International Monetary Fund and in the Australian federal departments of Finance, Foreign Affairs and Trade, The Treasury, and Prime Minister and Cabinet. He has also been Director of the APEC Study Centre at Griffith University, and Australian convener of the structural issues group of the Pacific Economic Cooperation Council (PECC).

Barry Maley was a Senior Fellow at the Centre for Independent Studies, and previously a Senior Lecturer in Behavioural Sciences at the University of New South Wales. Over his time with CIS, Barry wrote numerous books and policy monographs, including Family & Marriage in Australia,

Divorce Law and the Future of Marriage, and Family on the Edge, and published in excess of 150 opinion pieces in all major newspapers on a wide variety of topics. He was a Eureka Prize finalist in the field of 'Ethics' for his book *Divorce Law and the Future of Marriage* (2003). He was appointed to several professional advisory committees of the federal government, including the Australian Health Ethics Committee, 2006–08.

Nicholas Moore AO is a former Chief Executive Officer of Macquarie Group Limited. He retired in 2018 after 32 years at Macquarie, including 10 years as CEO. Nicholas has a Bachelor of Commerce and a Bachelor of Laws from the University of NSW. He was admitted as a solicitor and is a Fellow of the Institute of Chartered Accountants. In 2017, Nicholas was awarded an Honorary Doctorate in Business from UNSW. He is Chair of Screen Australia, The Centre for Independent Studies, The Smith Family, Willow Technology Corporation, the National Catholic Education Commission, the Financial Regulator Assessment Authority and the Markets Taskforce Expert Advisory Panel (within the Commonwealth Treasury) and Aldus Group. He is a member (and former Chair) of the UNSW Business School Advisory Council, a non-executive director of QBiotics Group, and a member of the Council of the National Gallery of Australia. In November 2022, Nicholas was appointed Special Envoy for Southeast Asia by the Commonwealth Government. He was previously Chair of the Sydney Opera House Trust, PCYC NSW, and has held directorships at Sydney Airport and Hills Motorway.

Terrence O'Brien is a former public servant who worked for some 40 years in the Commonwealth Treasury, Office of National Assessments, Productivity Commission and at the OECD and World Bank.

Michael Potter is Senior Economist at the Business Council of Australia, and previously a Senior Policy Manager at the Commonwealth Bank, a Policy Director at the Financial Services Council and a Research Fellow at the Centre for Independent Studies. Michael has worked for the Parliamentary Budget Office, the Federal Departments of Treasury, Environment and Prime Minister & Cabinet (where he advised then Prime Minister John Howard on the introduction of the GST). He has also worked as Policy Manager, Economics at the National Farmers' Federation, and

Director, Economics and Taxation at the Australian Chamber of Commerce and Industry. Michael has completed a Masters of Applied Economics from ANU and a Bachelor of Economics (Honours) from the University of Sydney.

Dr Alex Robson is Deputy Chair of the Productivity Commission, and an Adjunct Professor of Economics at QUT. He was formerly Professor of Economics at Griffith University, Australian Ambassador to the OECD, Chief Economist for the Australian Prime Minister, Associate Partner at EY, Director at Deloitte Access Economics, and Lecturer in Economics at the Australian National University. Author of Law and Markets. Consulted to ASX 200 companies, Australian and NZ Government Departments and the OECD. He holds a MA and PhD from the University of California.

Dr Jeremy Sammut holds a PhD in Australian political and social history from Monash University, and has published on historical topics including Australian federation, the WWI conscription referendums, the woman's suffrage movement, the White Australia Policy, immigration, multiculturalism, and Indigenous affairs. He was previously a Senior Research Fellow and the Director of the Culture, Prosperity and Civil Society Program at The Centre for Independent Studies, and is currently the leader writer and opinion editor for the *The Australian Financial Review*. He led the CIS Health research program for a decade and is a leading expert on market-based healthcare innovation and policy reform.

Professor Peter Saunders was formerly a Senior Fellow and Director of Social Policy at the Centre for Independent Studies, and Professor of Sociology at the University of Sussex in England and Research Manager at the Australian Institute of Family Studies. His work at the CIS focused mainly on issues of poverty, social inequality and welfare reform. His publications include *Remoralising the Welfare State, When Prophecy Fails, Social Foundations of a Free Society, A Self-Reliant Australia, Australia's Welfare Habit: And how to kick it*, and *The Government Giveth and the Government Taketh Away*. He also edited *Taxploitation: The Case for Income Tax Reform*.

Michael Stutchbury is the Executive Director of the Centre for Independent Studies, and the former Editor-in-Chief of *The Australian Financial Review*, a role he held from 2011 until 2024, when he became the masthead's Editor-at-Large. Before leading the *Financial Review*, he served as Economics Editor and later as Editor of *The Australian*, where he played a key role in shaping national discourse on fiscal policy, industrial relations, and economic reform. He graduated with a Bachelor of Economics (First Class Honours) from Adelaide University. His career has consistently demonstrated a strong grasp of the interplay between government policy and market dynamics, making him a prominent voice in debates over taxation, regulation, and productivity.

Tom Switzer was Executive Director of the Centre for Independent Studies from 2017-25. He is also a contributor to *The Australian*, the *Australian Financial Review* and Sky News Australia. From 2014 to 2023, he presented *Between the Lines* on the ABC's Radio National. He is also a former senior fellow at the University of Sydney's United States Studies Centre (2009-17), Australian editor of *The Spectator* in the UK (2009-14), opinion editor of *The Australian* (2001-08), editorial writer at the *Australian Financial Review* (1998-01) and assistant editor at the American Enterprise Institute in Washington, DC (1995-98). He graduated with a Bachelor of Arts in modern history (Hons) and a Master of Arts in international relations at the University of Sydney.

Matthew Taylor was the Director of the Intergenerational program at the CIS that focuses on intergenerational inequality and the fiscal burden of government policy on future generations. Previously to that, Matt held a research position at the Centre for Social Research and Methods at the Australian National University (ANU) and is currently a PhD candidate at the Crawford School of Public Policy at ANU. He was also previously at CIS from 2014 to 2015 working on paid parental leave and age pension policy. Matt has over a decade of experience in economic modelling and data analysis. Prior to joining CIS Matt worked for a number of government agencies and universities including the National Centre for Social and Economic Modelling at the University of Canberra, the Commonwealth Department of Employment and the Australian Institute of Family Studies.

Dr Peter Tulip is Chief Economist at the Centre for Independent Studies. He previously worked in the Research Department of the Reserve Bank of Australia and before that at the Federal Reserve Board of Governors. His recent research focuses on housing and monetary policy. He has a PhD from the University of Pennsylvania.

Gene Tunny is an Adjunct Scholar at the Centre for Independent Studies and Director of Adept Economics. He is a former Australian Treasury official who has managed teams in Treasury's Industry and Budget Policy divisions. In recent years, in addition to a wide range of domestic and international consulting projects, Gene has led several courses for foreign officials as part of University of Queensland International Development teams. Gene is a regular economics commentator in Australian and international media. He has a First Class Honours degree in economics from the University of Queensland. Gene is the current President of the Economic Society of Australia (QLD).

www.ingramcontent.com/pod-product-compliance
Ingram Content Group UK Ltd.
Pitfield, Milton Keynes, MK11 3LW, UK
UKHW020200290926
15471UKWH00005B/976

9 781923 568266